When Grief
Comes Home

When Grief Comes Home

A GENTLE GUIDE FOR LIVING THROUGH LOSS WHILE SUPPORTING YOUR CHILD

ERIN LEIGH NELSON AND
COLLEEN E. MONTAGUE, LMFT

BakerBooks
a division of Baker Publishing Group
Grand Rapids, Michigan

Published by Baker Books
a division of Baker Publishing Group
Grand Rapids, Michigan
BakerBooks.com

Printed in the United States of America

Library of Congress Cataloging-in-Publication Data
Names: Nelson, Erin L., author. | Montague, Colleen E., author.
Title: When grief comes home : a gentle guide for living through loss while supporting
    your child / Erin L. Nelson and Colleen E. Montague, LMFT.
Description: Grand Rapids, Michigan : Baker Books, a division of Baker Publishing
    Group, 2025. | Includes bibliographical references.
Identifiers: LCCN 2024023234 | ISBN 9781540904065 (paperback) | ISBN
    9781540904713 (casebound) | ISBN 9781493449088 (ebook)
Subjects: LCSH: Grief. | Bereavement. | Loss (Psychology)
Classification: LCC BF575.G7 N45 2025 | DDC 248.8/66—dc23/eng/20240603
LC record available at https://lccn.loc.gov/2024023234

Cover design by Greg Jackson, ThinkPen Design

Published in association with Books & Such Literary Management, www.booksandsuch.com

Baker Publishing Group publications use paper produced from sustainable forestry practices and postconsumer waste whenever possible.

25   26   27   28   29   30   31   7   6   5   4   3   2   1

CONTENTS

A Benediction   168

A WELCOMING

I (Erin) first entered the grief world on June 20, 1995, when a 3:00 a.m. phone call pushed me into a life I never imagined. The kids and I were visiting my in-laws in Monterey, California, a couple of hours from our home, while my husband, Tyler, was fishing in Alaska with his friends. My five-year-old daughter, Cassie, asleep in my bed, wrapped herself around me as I picked up the phone. Her grip tightened as I listened to my brother-in-law tell Tyler's parents and me that Tyler's plane had collided with another small plane on the way back to the lodge after fishing. There were no survivors.

I packed our bags and whispered, "No, no, no," as I pulled my sleeping three-year-old, Cody, out of bed, zipped his jacket over his footy pajamas, and buckled him into his car seat. While I drove home, I looked over the Monterey Valley farmland as the sun rose, and my terror mixed with a warm sense of peace. I wondered, Why are people going to work as if nothing happened? I thought tragic phone calls in the middle of the night only happened to other people. But grief had come home.

A few months later, my mom, who lived with bipolar disorder, suffered her third major depressive episode. She overdosed in an attempt to end her life, and soon after, she died. My fifteen-year-old sister, Kelli, came to live with the kids and me. The trauma of our mother's suicide deepened our fragility.

My inner light grew dim.

I moved through my days in a fog. Sometimes I had to remind myself to be alive even though I felt dead inside. Turn your head. Listen. Nod. Speak words back to the child asking you a question. At the same time, I was enchanted by the beauty of everyday mercies. Cassie's face when she was sleeping. Cody's little hands. The kindness of our neighbors.

And breath by breath, anchored in the support of others and by divine mercy, my light began to reemerge.

Finding a solid place to stand in my new life took time. I found ways to heal. Slowly I awakened to the mystery and paradox of post-traumatic growth—what had crushed me was expanding my soul, making room for beauty and life. Breaths turned into days, then months, and then years. I met a kindhearted man named Bryan from my church. He was a teacher and coach at a local high school who had offered to tutor my sister, Kelli, with her studies. We married and welcomed two more children, Carter and Camille, into our family.

I sensed a calling to learn how to support others through their losses and enrolled in classes on bereavement and childhood trauma. I learned about the Dougy Center in Portland, Oregon, the first grief center for children and families, which has inspired over five hundred grief peer support programs for children and families worldwide. Then in 2012, with a team of gifted professionals and volunteers, I helped launch Jessica's House, a grief center for children, teens, young adults, and parents in the Central Valley of California. Jessica's House has since supported thousands of children, teens, young adults, and parents through peer support and expressive arts.

Then, in 2019, facing the unimaginable felt impossible when my younger son, Carter, was in a car accident. The child who brought me so much joy after a season of devastation took his last breath surrounded by our family in the hospital. As I felt his last heartbeat with my hand on his chest, I wondered how mine kept beating.

I raged at God and doubted his goodness. Would our family survive another loss?

Early one morning, I texted my friend whose daughter had died several years earlier. I typed, "I'm falling into the darkness." She replied, "The darkness will hold you." And I remembered.

Once again, breath by breath, anchored in divine love and the support of others, my light is emerging.

And I am here to hold hope for you in whatever loss you face.

Breath by breath. As you find your way.

I f you are reading this book, a profound loss has touched your family. Your loved one has died. *Your* loved one. Grief has come home.

You are facing the unimaginable and left to mourn your own profound loss while also supporting your child through their grief. You may feel alone and unprepared. Through this book, we offer gentle reassurance and healing practices to help you feel supported and equipped to attend to your own grief so you can nurture your child's.

We wrote this book for you from our professional and personal experience. I (Erin) have the honor of serving families as the founding director of Jessica's House. My coauthor and colleague, Colleen Montague, is a licensed marriage and family therapist who has worked with families in crisis for over ten years. She is the director of outreach and education for Jessica's House. Together, we write resources for parents who are grieving a loss while raising their children and train professionals and first responders on how to support children and families in grief.

The chapters of this book cover topics you may face after the death of your loved one. You can choose to read cover to cover or flip to a topic that fits your specific needs. Each chapter begins with reflections from my personal grief experience and moves to our professional guidance for mourning while supporting your child. Through best practices for grief expression and thoughts from other parents who are grieving, we offer practical ways to honor your grief.

Chapters end with reflective questions and expressive activities for you and your child, with a closing blessing from my grieving heart to yours as you find ways to heal. At the end of the book, you will find a collection of resources for supporting your child, along with a section for you to share with *your* supporters on how they can be helpful companions to you.

After witnessing the anguish and courage of thousands of grievers, we are here to share what we've learned from children and parents living through the unimaginable. We pray these learnings will help you find your own way, in your own time. As you bear the unbearable with your family, we are here. Let's move through your loss together.

1

The Early Days

When we returned home from Monterey, family and friends were trick-ling in, and I still needed to tell Cody that his daddy had died. How could I say those words? The dad he welcomed home from work each day, the arms he ran to, would never again walk through the back door. I took Cody's hand and walked from the chaos of the house to the quietness of the backyard sandbox his daddy had built. We sat down, and I played in the sand alongside him, trying to find the words. I took a shaky breath.

"Cody, I need to tell you something."

He stopped playing and looked up at me.

"Your daddy was hurt in an accident. His plane hit another plane, and his body stopped working. He died because of how hurt he was."

He crashed his toys together.

"Was it like this? Or like that?" he asked, banging them in different directions.

Later that day, after hearing someone say his daddy was in heaven, Cody and I were back to the quiet of the sandbox when he looked up at the roof of our home and said, "Mommy, what if we put a ladder on the roof and bring Daddy down?"

I looked over at the top of the house.

"I wish we could get a ladder and stretch so high and bring him down," I said.

I was learning to join his wishes and wonderings. I had my own.

While I was driving one day, Cassie said from the back seat, "Maybe Daddy's pilot was thirsty, and he reached down to get a drink and didn't see the other plane."

"Maybe he was," I said.

W ill we be okay?" is a common question when parents come to Jessica's House for the first time after their loss. You may be wondering that too. How did you get here? And how can you face your life without your loved one? Early grief often feels scary and unpredictable. You are living in the unimaginable.

The shock and confusion of their death, the replaying of what went wrong and how it could have been different loops like a movie in your mind. You may feel like your person dies again every morning when you wake up. Even if you slept only briefly, you wake up and remember. *It really happened . . . to US.*

You will survive your loss, though it may be hard to imagine that could be true right now. You will not only survive but learn to live in what remains. It's not how you want it to be. Every part of you will protest facing life without them. Yet somehow, mercy will meet you in ways you never imagined.

First, dear reader, press your hand over your heart. Take a moment now to take a deep breath in. Now let it out. As you face the unimaginable, know you will get through, moment by moment, breath by breath.

Everyone Grieves Differently

Each person's grief is as unique as their fingerprint, so as you move through your loss with your family, remember that each of you will grieve in your own distinct way. There is no right or wrong approach. One child may have an intense grief reaction while another doesn't. One may want to talk about the loss while another wants a break. The early days of grief are a good time to discuss your needs openly and give permission for each other to express yourselves uniquely. You will find ways to get through your loss together as you honor one another's needs of mourning.

You may be asking, "Is it okay for me to cry in front of my child?" Know that crying with your child models healthy mourning. You may be tempted to mask your emotions, but your honest expression with tears communicates how you miss your person and validates your child's feelings of loss. When you model your emotions by expressing them in front of your child, you give them permission to honestly express themselves with you. Doing this early in your grief process helps you build trust for active and authentic mourning together.

Visitors

Grief is a time for you to conserve your limited energy. One dad said, "I needed a quiet house after my wife died. Too many visitors felt like chaos." After her husband died, one mom voiced, "I needed someone to stay with me through my days and nights. Being alone was too much." If too many visitors deplete you, limiting them will help you invest energy in your own well-being. For example, you can ask those who want to help to drop off items at the door instead of coming in. One mom said, "Someone dropped off an ice chest filled with drinks on our porch and returned each day to add more drinks and replenish the ice. Having drinks on hand was a gift with all the visitors."

Consider what a safe and healthy support person looks like for you. Who can help you hold the weight of decision-making during such a tender time? When choosing who you want with you, ask yourself, *Does this person bring me energy or deplete it?*

Sensory Reminders

You and your child may notice distressing reminders about the death. Images like the physical decline of your loved one or an accident scene may replay in your mind. Such imagery is expected as your brain works to understand what happened, even if you were not present at the time of their death. These images help your brain process what occurred and become part of your future survival.[1] Your brain is doing what it was created to do: take care of you. You may also experience the replaying of sounds such as end-of-life breathing patterns related to your loved one's last moments. Images and other sensory reminders often reduce after a few weeks, and professional support can help if they persist.

After experiencing trauma, encountering reminders of the event through sounds, smells, and sights can cause your brain and body to react as if the event is happening in the current moment, sending you into a freeze, flight, or fight reaction. You may notice your heart is racing or your breathing is shallow. You can bring yourself back to your body through deep breathing and grounding.[2] One grounding technique is to press both feet to the floor while engaging your senses with three objects you see, two sounds you hear, and one scent you smell. Other options include sipping cold water, tapping your arms and legs, and rubbing your hands together then pressing them lightly over your eyes. These practices help bring you into the present moment, taking you out of your past experience.

Another way to cope with imagery is to look at photos of when your loved one was healthy or to visualize a place where you feel calm while swaying from side to side. One mom said it helped to watch her favorite comforting show on repeat. Another said she watched videos of puppies to give her brain a break from the images playing in her head.

Your Child's Grief Reactions

You may notice a shift in your child's behavior. They may express themselves with tears, angry outbursts, withdrawing, or wanting to be close to you. They may develop new fears of losing someone else and worry for your well-being or their own. Provide reassurance by explaining what you're doing to take good care of yourself, reminding them that what happened is rare, and assuring them you're doing all you can to keep them and yourself safe.

You will notice grief's impact in physical, cognitive, and emotional ways. Your child's physical reactions can include being tired or unable to sleep. They may have headaches, stomachaches, or an increased or decreased appetite. They may push family rule boundaries or return to habits that brought them comfort when they were younger, like thumb-sucking.[3] Their outward reactions communicate their inner world. Concentrating at school or home may be difficult. One child said, "I felt like someone opened my brain and poured in oatmeal." Another said, "I can see my teacher talking, but I can't understand what she is saying."

Complex emotional reactions like anger, guilt, relief, confusion, and disbelief are common and can be felt all at once. Your child's responses may show, or they may not. One child whose dad died said, "Sometimes I am sad because my dad isn't here. At the same time, I'm happy when I get to play with my cousin. I like to call it feeling 'sappy.'" Your child may not externally show their emotions through tears. After his dad died, one teen said, "I feel guilty because everyone cries a lot, but I can't." He added, "It's not that I don't care."

It's possible to experience a full spectrum of emotions in grief. The capacity to feel opposite emotions at the same time is a gauge of your mental health.[4] You can feel sadness and relief at the same time. Normalizing paradoxical emotions by admitting your own counters any shame your child may feel about their conflicting feelings. You can say, "I miss Daddy so much, and I also feel relieved that his body isn't in pain anymore. It feels weird to have two feelings at the same time. I'm wondering if you feel like that sometimes too."

It's natural for your child to wonder if they caused the death somehow and regret their words or actions. These new feelings can be scary and confusing. You can communicate your intention of wanting to know their questions by asking, "I'm wondering, what are you wondering?" They may doubt the death happened or believe they can somehow bring their person back to life. Reflective listening—where you use their words as a response—helps them feel understood. For example, if your child says, "Maybe if I had been with Daddy when the accident happened, I could have saved him," you could respond, "You're wondering if you could have saved your daddy if you were with him."

Being with them as they express their wishes in the early days builds trust for them to express their thoughts to you. You can't fix it. But your compassionate presence and openhearted listening promote their healing.

Supporting Your Child

It's common for children to feel a shift in their sense of security when a caregiver has died. You can bring stability to your child in the early days with consistent mealtimes and bedtimes. Tell them who will now fill the caregiving roles once held by their person, such as taking them to school or making meals. If their parent who died was the one who normally put them to bed, discuss what bedtime routines will be like now. Allow for choices when possible, including asking them what parts of the process they'd like to continue, such as reading a book or singing a song. Ensure your child can access items like their favorite stuffed animals or blanket, or perhaps something that links them to their person.

If their sibling died and they shared a bedroom, plan together the new sleeping arrangements that feel best. Some children ask to sleep in their parents' bed or on their bedroom floor after a death.

Allowing physical closeness during the days *and* nights helps foster comfort. One mom said, "After our young son died, our daughter, who shared a room with him, slept with my husband and me. After a few months, we switched our bedrooms. She stayed in our room, and we moved to theirs." Your physical presence is the best gift you can offer right now.

Ask your child what questions they have about how the person died and what they already know about the death. You may not have answers to their questions, but you can join them in their wonderings. If they ask, "Can Mommy see me from heaven?" you could respond, "You're wondering if Mommy can see you from heaven. What do you think?" Listen to their thoughts and ideas and share yours. Again, reflecting their ideas, thoughts, and emotions by restating what you hear them say helps them feel understood. As you reflect your child's words, also mirror their energy, facial expressions, and body language. Reflecting with mirroring helps them feel your attunement. If your child says in anger, "I'm so mad the doctors couldn't save my dad," you might respond with similar intensity, "You're angry there was nothing else the doctors could do. You wish they could have saved him."

For more information on explaining death to your child, turn to the resources section at the end of this book.

Taking Care of You

Grief has a natural way of slowing you down, so you won't always have the capacity for the tasks you once did. You may notice your thoughts feel muddled, and it is difficult to make decisions. Your energy level and capacity for family and friends may be low. You might find it difficult to take care of your own needs with the demands of caring for your child. Yet, just like the flight attendant who reminds you to place your oxygen mask on yourself before you put one on your child, taking care of yourself is what you need right now. A good practice is to continue to see your doctor for regular checkups to take good care of your physical and emotional health.

Honor the wisdom of your body. When you feel tired, rest. Eat healthy meals, drink water, and walk outdoors to help you to your next moment. You are experiencing a profound time of loss, and you are surviving.

Hand over heart, dear reader. Take a deep breath in.
Let it out. Say aloud, "I give myself
the compassion I need as I remember
I won't always feel the way I do right now."

HEALING PRACTICES

Reflection

CARE is an acronym to help you care for yourself in the early days.
In what ways can you:

Care for your body with healthy food, water, and movement
like stretching or walking outdoors?

Accept support in the ways you find most helpful?

Rest often and keep normal routines as much as possible?

Express your emotions with others as they arise?

Expressive Arts Invitation: Wishing Flags

Supplies needed: paper and markers

Invite your child to explore these prompts through writing words
or drawing images or designs:

I wonder . . .

I wish . . .

I hope . . .

*For examples of this and other expressive arts practices throughout
the book, visit JessicasHouse.org.*

Discussion Questions with Your Child

1. What are you wondering about?

2. What is a wish you have for your future?

Hot Cocoa Breathing for You and Your Child

- Visualize holding a cup of hot cocoa by cupping your hands together. Imagine feeling the warmth in your hands.
- Bring your "cup" to your nose and "smell" the hot cocoa by inhaling through your nose to the count of 1 . . . 2 . . . 3 . . . 4.
- Hold your breath 1 . . . 2 . . . 3 . . . 4 . . . 5 . . . 6 . . . 7 while imagining the smell of the chocolate.
- Slowly breathe out through your mouth 1 . . . 2 . . . 3 . . . 4 . . . 5 . . . 6 . . . 7 . . . 8, pretending to blow on the hot cocoa to cool it down.
- Repeat three times for a sense of calm.

Connections with Your Child in the Early Days

Morning

Provide physical closeness and touch.

Tell your child what their day will hold.

After school or being apart

Your child may have feelings they have been holding inside, so give them time to share tears or other emotions.

Play on the floor.

Talk about your "roses" and "thorns" (the best and worst parts of your day).

Go for a walk or bike ride together.

Bedtime

Provide physical closeness and touch.

Offer a back scratch.

Review what you look forward to the next day—it can be as simple as a friend's visit or time playing outside.

A Blessing in the Wishes and Wonderings

When you wonder

When did the world stop being your shelter?
And how does it move from night to day?

When in the morning they are still gone

How does the sun still shine?
And the birds still sing?
Why are the flowers blooming?

And WHY?
Was there no protection?

No healing?
When you stand in the ruins
And can't find home

May you be met
With stubborn companions
And know you will be held

2

Opening to Your Sorrow

Seven months after Tyler's death, my mom, who lived with bipolar disorder, died of suicide. She was playful, gentle, empathetic, thoughtful, and wickedly funny. She was smart and accomplished—a nurse whose lifework was caring for babies in the NICU. And I wanted to remember all of her. The way she scooped up spiders to release them outside and how she slapped her knee when she laughed. But the way she died seemed to overshadow the splendor of who she was.

C. S. Lewis once said he didn't know that grief felt so much like fear.[1] That was true for me after Tyler died; I lived with a feeling of emptiness and dread.

But after my mom's suicide, my emptiness filled with shame.

I noticed others' reticence in speaking about her and relating to me. There were awkward conversations in church corridors and diversions at grocery stores.

As the months went by, my inner spark grew dim. The complexity of enduring another loss and grieving a stigmatized death increased my fragility. The night welcomed me—a haunting invitation that led to new life.

I lived with an ongoing image of God leading me in the darkness from behind. His holy hands on my shoulders were a gentle guide. We walked *together down a hallway in an unfamiliar home. I saw light radiating from beneath the doors of each room.*

Sometimes, God would crack open a door, granting me a glimpse into divine provision—the illumination of sacred possibilities.

Your loss invites you to be with your pain. In a culture that values hustle and good vibes only, attuning to mourning is not something we do well. You open to your sorrow as you allow and express your full spectrum of emotions and invite your grief to follow a natural flow of expansion and contraction. Just as your body knows how to heal a broken bone, it knows how to heal your broken heart. As you ebb and flow through the range of your feelings at a pace that feels best for you, trust in your natural capacity to heal. Grief carries momentum to the dark and tender places, inviting you to where new life begins.

Episcopal priest and author Barbara Brown Taylor writes, "New life starts in the dark. Whether it's a seed in the ground, a baby in the womb, or Jesus in the tomb, it starts in the dark."[2] As you open to your sorrow, notice the energy of grief in your body. As the sensations of your emotions build, what needs to be outwardly expressed? When your feelings are both felt and expressed, you complete the cycle of their purpose, which is to restore the balance of your nervous system, bringing you back to your "just-right" place. As you protest your loss and yearn for what you wish had been, you may find relief through crying, talking, walking, yoga, writing, punching the air, or screaming. The more you attune to your body and allow the flow of your restoration cycle to have full expression, the more relief and release you'll find.

As a parent, when you ride your natural rhythm of grief and expression of both darkness and light, you are modeling mourning for your child. Parents often share that they don't want to be sad in front of their children. Yet children are keen at sensing their caregivers' emotions. Suppressing your grief and pretending you are okay contradicts their intuition that something isn't right, hindering your child's ability to develop and rely on their own instincts. As you authentically grieve in front of your child, you validate your shared grief and lessen their confusion.

Your Earliest Modeling of Grief

Take a moment to reflect on how others modeled grieving for you growing up. What types of emotional expression were welcome in your family? Which feelings felt risky to express? Which emotions were labeled as "bad"? Which feelings were you afraid to feel?

Recognizing your family's patterns can help you better understand your responses to loss. Some families lean into their losses and are active participants in their grief. Others may steer away from the pain or hold the mindset "We need to move on." Perhaps your family's cultural practices were unsupportive of an outward expression of grief. Which of your family's ways of grieving do you find helpful? Which ones are unhelpful? You can choose how you model grief for your child as you companion their grief and attend to your own.

Grief's Golden Hour

When your child was born, they had a "golden hour" after they went from the dark, warm, safe, predictable world of the womb to your arms. Your baby was alert and ready to bond with you during that golden hour. Research shows that skin-to-skin contact during this period stabilizes their distress and reduces their risks for complications.[3]

And just like the golden hour with your newborn, there is a valuable time to be with your grief after your loss. Your golden hour isn't about a specific time frame but rather how you are with your grief as it arises. Often, in the early days after loss, the intensity of your grief demands you embrace what needs to be seen and felt at a pace that is right for you. You don't have to feel it all at once. Grief comes to you in bits and pieces and at the most unexpected times. Whatever presents itself asks to be noticed and attended to *right now* because it may never come again in the same way.

In these early days of grief, you have limitations and a different capacity of what you can hold. You are not broken, but you *are* brokenhearted. You can no longer keep to the schedule or manage the responsibilities in the ways you once did. You are learning your new way of being. Your golden hour is when you attune to what you need and teach others about the new you. Trust the truth of the messages your body sends you; bodies never lie. Just as the pain of birth is transformative—making space for new life—you are transforming now in the pain of your grief. You heal as you notice and express what you are sensing, putting the needs of your body first, always.

And just like a woman who has given birth, you need extra rest, help, gentleness, and grace as you learn your new way of life. Physician and UCSF medical educator Rachel Remen writes, "Every great loss demands that we choose life again. We need to grieve in order to do this. The pain we have not grieved over will always stand between us and life."[4]

To someday remember with love and pain requires your full presence in your golden hour. Being born into your new world of grief is a stark contrast to holding your baby for the first time, yet it still needs your full attention. When you first held your child in your arms, whether at birth or later in their life, you were wholly engaged as you discovered every part of them. The folds in their ears, their eyelashes, their fingers and toes. It's the same with your grief. Your attention to mourning allows you to integrate your loss.

The Risks of Avoidance

Because your brain is wired to avoid pain, there will be times when you want to suppress your emerging feelings of grief. But notice if your avoidance continues with denial, distraction, or numbing. It might show up as busyness, overdrinking, overeating, substance misuse, excessive exercise, or avoiding people or activities that remind you of your loss.[5] One mom, who had jumped into the role of a suicide-prevention activist after the loss of her son by suicide, later expressed, "I wish I had waited before working so hard to champion a cause. Now I see I missed a vital time of healing when my son's death was at the top of the minds of others who wanted to be with me in my pain. I can't go back, and now everyone has moved on." Part of your healing may include advocacy or helping others, but allowing those things to come only when you have the capacity helps reserve your limited energy for your healing during this unique time.

Numbing or distracting from grief cuts short the fullness of your healing. Seek to engage with just 10 percent of your pain, then go back to a place of nurturing yourself. You can try to nurture yourself by wrapping your left hand under your right arm, then wrapping your right arm around the top of your left arm. Squeeze your left shoulder with your right hand. Stay there, adding the pressure you need with your touch, until you notice you can take a deeper breath.

Some situations may prevent you from being with your grief in those early days. Perhaps you had to return to work after a brief bereavement leave during which you were consumed with funeral planning and other logistic needs. Caring for other family members, especially children, can also require much of your energy and focus. However, it's never too late. Your attention, at the time and pace right for you, builds a path for healthy integration of your loss.

Circumstances of the Death

As you open to your sorrow, another layer to your grief may be the circumstances surrounding the death. One dad said, "The nurses and chaplains were so compassionate during my daughter's death. Their empathy gave us strength. We saw how hard they tried and how much they cared." Another voiced, "When our son died, it was so chaotic, we felt like we weren't given the information we needed. Hospital staff were cold, and it didn't seem like they were doing everything they could to help him or us. After he died, we were left standing in the hallway alone and told we couldn't leave until we gave them the name of the funeral home so they could take his body. The hospital experience added to the trauma of losing him."

If your loved one lived with a life-limiting illness and you were their caregiver, you may have been grieving even before the death. One mom said, "For years, my time was mostly spent caregiving for my husband. I invested my love and energy in him. There is a part of me that is relieved that he's no longer in pain and I no longer have the stress of his care. Another part of me walks around wondering, 'What do I do now?'"

Supporting Your Child

Children often move in and out of their grief. They are natural mourners and organically follow their own rhythm of healing. In one moment they may ask questions about the death and the next go play outside. They may have an outburst of anger one minute and laugh the next. Or your child may show a lack of feelings in response to the death. Their brain is protecting them from the full weight of the loss while making room for healing. Like you, they can hold the darkness and light at the same time. One facet of being a companion for your child is honoring their defenses. As grief educator Alan Wolfelt describes, "Never force [your child] to feel something before they are ready for the pain that precedes healing."[6]

Trust that your child will move toward their new reality in their own time. Just like you have the natural ability to heal, so does your child. While their grief may not always be visible, their process is germinating under the surface, like a seed. As they witness you expressing your grief, you invite them to open to theirs.

Be a student of how they're mourning. Let them teach you what they need. They will notice your desire to understand. Your empathy offers them permission to feel, express, and be.

Finding Your New Self

You will find your new self in bits and pieces as you grieve in bits and pieces. Trust that your brain knows how to soften the impact of your loss so you don't absorb it all at once. Open yourself to what you're feeling right now and express that energy as you feel it. You might scream, let out a forceful breath, or cry. And just like rivers need to flow, your unhindered tears will loosen what needs release. You are creating a new way of being in the world, and your mourning makes room for your discovery. The way you mourn determines how you will live and thrive. You are moving toward remembering with love and pain and not just pain.

Your path from survivor to thriver means you continue to find ways to keep the flow of your expression of grief. It's not about returning to your former self. It's about finding grace as you become your new self.

Hand over heart, dear reader. Deep breath in.
Let it out. Say aloud, "I give myself the compassion
I need as I trust my natural way of grieving."

HEALING PRACTICES

Reflection

1. What helps you open to the full spectrum of your emotions?
2. What does avoiding your grief look like for you?
3. What type of expression brings you relief?

Expressive Arts Invitation: Sources of Strength

Supplies needed: paper and writing utensils

Each person in the family creates a personalized list of activities that bring them strength. Post these lists in your home to review them when needed. Ideas include spending time with a friend, watching the sunrise, going to a movie, practicing yoga, spending time with a pet, playing a sport, coloring, or going for a walk.

Discussion Questions with Your Child

1. Who is someone who helps you feel strong?
2. Which of the activities you listed brings you the most strength?

A Blessing for When Your Light Grows Dim

When your light grows dim
And the darkness shrouds you
Like stubborn fog

When you are afraid
You will be in grief's tentacles the rest of your days

May divine light
Help you find yourself
The part of you that is yet to be
Yes
You are shrouded in darkness now

But there is always a spark

And the who of you
The true of you
Is becoming

3

When You're Grieving Your Partner

I pulled on the cart until it came unstuck from the one in front of it, backed up a few steps, and then turned to steer through the sliding doors of our neighborhood market. It was my first time facing a grocery run since Tyler died.

Turning down the aisle, I reached for his favorite cookies—the pink and white iced animal ones with sprinkles. But then I remembered . . . no one liked those but him.

I left my empty cart in the aisle and returned to my car, wondering, What do I buy at the store now that he's gone? *I always had him in mind when I planned family meals. It was fun to make his favorites. Cooking dinner now seemed useless.*

And who knew I made decisions with him in mind in almost every part of my life? We worked together in our family business, so he **was** *my every day. We were a team running the company together. And I was a farmer's wife. A wife.*

Who was I now, without him?

I lived with a constant urge throughout my days to call and tell him what was happening with the kids and to ask him what I should do with all the decisions I needed to make. But mostly this: "Oh, hey, I'm just calling to tell you something awful happened. You died."

T he definition of *bereaved* is "torn apart."[1] If your partner or spouse died, part of *you* also died *with* them because part of them lived in you and you in them. You are torn apart from them, and you may feel like you are both physically and emotionally torn apart too. You knew them (as they knew you) in ways few understand, with a shared history, memories, and interactions that now belong to only you. You grieve for what you lost, what you never had, and what you hoped for your future.

The Loss of Your Companion

When your partner dies, you face the profound loss of the one who held everyday life with you. One mom said, "When my husband died, it felt like someone broke into my home and robbed me of my hopes and dreams. My life is not what I thought it would be." Grieving your partner is one of the most disorienting experiences you can face. One mom said when her husband died, she felt dizzy, like her whole world was off balance. Her partner was her safe place, her best friend. She said, "We met when we were teenagers. He was the only life I had ever known."

Rhythms and routines anchored your days together. With those comforts stripped away, you may feel untethered. One dad said, "My wife and I were in the middle of our favorite TV series when she died. I can't bring myself to finish it without her." A wife whose husband died said, "I miss our nightly check-ins about our days. I started writing short notes to him in my journal about the highlights, asking him questions, wondering what he would say about the new happenings in my life. It's not the same, but it helps."

You went from sharing a household and raising children together to holding it solo. The weight of assuming both roles can feel impossible. One mom commented, "I don't have as much time for a social life now because I have more responsibilities as the solo parent. Now I'm mowing the lawn, taking out the garbage, and getting the car serviced. All the tasks my husband once did." One dad mentioned that along with yearning for his partner, he also missed dividing the load of life's responsibilities with her. He now feels the pressure of being fully responsible for raising their children and longs for the days when he shared everyday decision-making with her. "I don't want to be the only one who messes up our kids," he added with a wink.

Your sense of searching and yearning stems from the connection you shared and the unwanted reality of their physical absence in your life. One mom said, "Some nights I found myself waiting for my husband to walk through the door. When I saw a car resembling his, I thought, 'There he is!' It felt like a trick when he wasn't in the driver's seat." One day, after smelling his wife's perfume while shopping, one dad said, "I caught the scent and began searching for my wife, and somehow I thought, maybe, just maybe, it's her."

Together you built a life, shaped by shared values and traditions. While the same values may remain, what happens to the traditions? One mom, whose family took yearly summer vacations to the mountains, wondered what she should do now with her husband gone. Searching for some normalcy, she decided to go to the mountains, but she said, "The kids and I found it too hard to be there without him. We dreamed of where we would go if we chose someplace new and decided to go to the beach next time. Maybe we'll try the mountains again someday when it seems right."

When your partner was alive, the needs of your family, work, school, home maintenance, and extended relationships created a daily routine. Consumed by the needs of everyday life, you weren't thinking you might have limited time together. Because you are

33

human, you likely offended them at times, and they did the same. In life, we are disappointed and we disappoint. We are failed and we fail. Mercy and grace are gifts we learn to give ourselves and each other in life, but especially in death.

Regret after the death of a spouse or partner is a natural part of grief.[2] If you were to express your "woulda, coulda, shouldas" and what-ifs to others who have experienced a loss like yours, you would find you are not alone. Because relationships are a constant source of challenge and nurturing, you were in the middle of a process that never fully matured. You may wish you could have shared more and loved better. One mom voiced, "After my husband died, I stayed in 'marriage counseling.' Before he died, we were in the middle of moving through tough issues with our counselor. I began to understand my husband even more after his death and saw our relationship in a new way."

There may be aspects of your relationship with your person that you don't miss. Even in the best of relationships, some quirks and habits annoy us. After someone dies, it may feel wrong to acknowledge your person's imperfections and struggles, but being honest can help you grieve more authentically. Some of what others say about your person may not feel true to you. There are likely parts of your loved one's life (like everyone's) that won't make it into the eulogy. When you acknowledge their fallibility, it doesn't make them less worthy of your celebration; rather, you are bringing honor to the wholeness of their story and the darkness and light of humanity.

Social Changes

When your partner dies, dynamics with others in the family and your community can shift, leaving you feeling socially isolated. One mom described it as "a tornado that swooped me up and turned me around, dropping me into a foreign land." You may ache to go "home" to the familiar. Just like Dorothy in *The Wizard of Oz*, who said, "I can't go back the way I came," you may want to go back to your life as it once was but are finding the only way to the other side is through.

The death of your spouse may also be the death of another's sibling or child. Each is mourning their relationship and may encounter a repeated sense of disbelief that the person is really gone. The ache to return to when your loved one was alive surfaces at different times for each person in the family. You will notice how each individual is at a different place at different times as they encounter the brewing, peaking, and receding of their grief reactions. These patterns keep grief reactions active and add to the complexity of family members feeling tangled emotions at various times, potentially fueling a cycle of misunderstandings.

Another area that may be impacted by the death of your partner is your social life. You may notice shifts in your relationships with extended family and friends. One mom shared how her friendships had changed since her husband died, saying, "I've noticed an unfamiliar, lonely feeling with my friends." Another mom whose husband died from a long-term illness said that the demands of his care left her with little time to invest in her friends. She explained, "After his death, I found it awkward to reengage with some of my married friends. I wondered if they didn't know what to say when I was around." She later began seeking traveling and hiking adventures with a new group of friends. At times she found relief in spending time with others who didn't share a history with her.

Decision-Making

Losing a partner also means facing financial decisions you never imagined you would need to make without them. Finding a team of professionals and trusted friends can help you as you make choices for your financial future. One dad whose wife died said that a fellow bereaved friend told him not to make big purchases in the first year after her death, and that helped stabilize the kids and him. He said, "I had an urge to buy something new to make myself feel better, but that advice helped me make better decisions." Another mom said, "I felt guilty taking insurance money because it seemed like I was benefiting from my husband's death somehow. I didn't want the money. I wanted *him*." A dad whose wife once handled all the finances found it challenging to manage household responsibilities alongside paying the bills and doing the banking. He said, "The best decision I made was to find others to help me with my finances."

Supporting Your Child

When a parent dies, children lose a sense of control. They can feel confused by the unfamiliar emotions they are experiencing. Sharing information about the death as you receive it invites your child to the process, lending them a sense of control. Telling your child that you will be the one to inform them of new findings about the death helps them look to you as a source of truth and information. When facts are left to their imagination or given by peers or others in the family, they may adopt misconceptions that are difficult to untangle.

You can support your child's sense of safety with routines, your physical proximity, listening, and touch. Remind them you aren't afraid of their emotions, and expressing their feelings is healthy. You can provide comfort through listening with an empathetic head tilt, leaning in, slowing your breathing, and placing your hand on your child's back with gentle pressure to create a sense of physical support.

Another way to create safety is to intentionally provide predictability by limiting change in their life when possible. You may need to overcommunicate for a time and let them know in advance if there are unexpected shifts in plans for their day. If you do have to make a change to your child's school, your work, or your home, have age-appropriate discussions to help them feel *part* of the change rather than feel it is happening *to* them. If you must make a big transition like a move, maintain the same family rules, schedules, and chores to foster a sense of security.

The death of a parent fractures a child's sense of safety. Discussing who will take care of them if something happens to you can ease their worries. Reassure them that you plan to live for a long time and that you are taking good care of yourself to help make that happen.

You Don't Have to Hold Your Grief Alone

As you carry the loss of your partner, look for others who can support you. Seek others to be with you who can hold your story about what happened to your partner, what it's like for you to live without them, and the challenges of solo parenting. Keep sharing stories about your partner with your child and find ways to remember them.

Hand over heart, dear reader.
Deep breath in. Let it out. Say aloud,
"May I be kind to myself as I find my way."

HEALING PRACTICES

Reflection

Write a letter to your partner using these phrases:

I miss the times we _____ .
I'll never forget _____ .
I see you in the kids when _____ .
Thank you for _____ .

Expressive Arts Invitation: A Memory in My Hand

Supplies needed: paper and markers, colored pencils, or oil pastels

Each person in the family traces one hand on their piece of paper. In the palm of your drawn hand, illustrate your favorite memory with your loved one who died. Think about what you noticed with your five senses in your memory. What was the weather like? What did the air feel like on your skin? What did you see? What did you hear? What did you taste? What did you smell? Write or draw what you saw, felt, heard, tasted, and smelled, using one finger for each sense.

Discussion Questions with Your Child

1. If you could change one part of your memory with your loved one, what would it be?
2. If you could relive one part of your memory with your loved one, what would it be?

A Blessing in the Longing

When the cadence of your life
What once was a parallel melody
Is now the anthem of your heart longing
For the timbre of what was
May you know
That you bear inside you a song
A divine ballad
A refrain
Reminding you
Love is here

4

When You're Grieving Your Child

I remember talking to friends and family at Carter's viewing at the funeral home. I told them that even if they face the biggest fear of their whole lives, they won't die.

I could not believe my heart could still beat after his stopped. And somehow, morning after morning, I kept waking up. And his room was still empty. What I had always feared might happen, happened.

Didn't I read Runaway Bunny to Carter when he was young? Didn't I promise I would always find him? But he's everywhere and nowhere. My love goes out to find my home in him and then returns to me, crushing my bones. He is gone.

I live with a constant overshadow of missing him. Like the orca who carried her dead calf for a thousand miles, I am carrying him.[1] And he is worth every tear, every scream, every call of my heart, "Come back!"

It's a love song.

I f your child died, you are left holding the enormity of everything you'll face with them missing from all of your tomorrows. Your love for your child is shaped only for them. It can't relocate. There's nowhere for it to go, and you are left longing for their presence. Studies on bereaved parents show that yearning is a primary emotional response after losing a child.[2] You are living with *Sehnsucht*, a German word defined as "an ongoing intense and painful desire for something that is not attainable or far away."[3] As poet Edward Hirsch wrote after losing his son:

> I did not know the work of mourning
> Is like carrying a bag of cement
> Up a mountain at night
> The mountaintop is not in sight
> Because there is no mountaintop[4]

The only remedy for the pain of losing your child is to grieve their physical absence in your life. The agony you feel must be expressed to the depths you feel it. When words aren't enough to describe your yearning, scream, moan, cry, and breathe. A loss this profound is only healed breath by breath. Your other children are healing alongside you, and your honest expression of yearning affirms their feelings of loss.[5]

Changes in Your Family

Sibling dynamics are affected as each child in your family has a distinct role and brings a unique energy to your home and world. You may have lost the funny one, the one who gathered the family around music or sports, or the one who loved art. Perhaps the oldest became the only child, or the middle child became the oldest or youngest. You may have always considered your family a party of four, and now you are a party of three.

You may need to respond to tough questions like, "How many children do you have?" One mom mentioned she always says the number of her children, adding, "One is in heaven." She continued, "Sometimes the person will apologize for bringing it up, and I've found the best response for me is to say, 'I like to talk about him.'" When asked, "How old are they?" one dad said, "I say I have two living children, ten and thirteen." Others say it depends on the circumstance, and sometimes it's too hard to talk about in the moment. Thinking ahead on how you wish to answer these questions helps lessen the fear of how to respond. If the question exceeds your capacity to answer, you aren't dishonoring your child; you are attending to your needs at that moment.

After the death of your child, it may be hard to be with other family members or friends with children the same age as yours. One mom shared how her relationship with her sister changed, adding, "She didn't understand my grief's complexity or that it's forever. She didn't ask about my grief for my daughter. She wanted me to feel better. My child loss support group friends are the only ones who understand."

Relationship with Your Partner

If you're with your partner, the despair that comes with losing your child impacts your relationship. You are both grieving your child alongside the stress of everyday life. Additional stressors after your child dies include medical bills, funeral costs, worrying about your other children, and wondering how you will function at work and home.

You and your partner are grieving the loss of your child together and separately. Your grief needs are uniquely yours and always changing. Your grief is different from your partner's. You will face "grief storms" at contrasting times, making it difficult to find your usual rhythms. Allow space for the tears, the shared silence, and even exploring the what-ifs. Keep communicating what you need. You weren't mind readers before, and now you are faced with the unknowns and pain of one of life's most profound losses.

Carry your grief together and with others. Your loss is too much to hold alone or just between the two of you. Seeking support outside one another helps both of you feel surrounded by the layers of reinforcement you need.

Because each of you had a distinct relationship with your child, you may feel the intensity of your pain differently. Your differences can lead to misunderstandings and feeling misheard. It's natural for one spouse to feel like they are hurting more than the other at times. With your reserves depleted, emotions will trump all reasoning, leaving you with raw and unfiltered reactions. Look for opportunities to connect in small ways, even if it seems trite, such as watching a lighthearted show together or taking a walk. In her book *Rare Bird: A Memoir of Loss and Love*, bereaved mom Ann Whiston-Donaldson says, "That our marriage has survived, and will continue to survive such devastation, feels to me like something of a miracle, and I don't take it for granted. Each day is a new opportunity to show each other grace."[6]

Intimacy Alongside Grief

A topic often not discussed openly is intimacy after the loss of a child. Because the nature of your loss is consuming and exhausting, intimacy, including sex, may not be something you desire or have the capacity for. You may find it difficult to embrace intimacy alongside the intensity of your emotions. The pleasure of sex may feel wrong or irreverent to you, or it may be something you find very comforting.

The complexity of grief adds to the intricacy of your body. Because your brain is affected by the loss and trauma you experienced, you don't feel like yourself. Feelings of disinterest can lead to more complicated reactions of guilt. Be gentle with yourself and trust that your outlook around intimacy after child loss is evolving.

Be open and honest with your partner about how you feel and when you feel ready for intimacy. Explore other ways to connect that don't involve sex. Relating in ways that feel comfortable for each person tends to your needs during the isolation of grief. Try holding hands or simply sitting close together. Make eye contact in your conversations. Just as grief holds no time limit, there is no timeline for returning to intimacy. Simply surviving the loss of a child together is its own form of communion.

There are false statistics about bereaved parents touting that up to 90 percent of marriages of parents who lose a child will end in divorce. Yet recent research shows that only 16 percent of marriages end after the death of a child.[7] This statistic is below the national average and points to how relationships can be strengthened when you go through the trauma of losing a child together. Your shared memories of your child and how you found ways to get through it with each other will forever be part of your family history.

Supporting Your Child

Supporting your child after the death of their sibling may feel impossible. You are shattered by the profound loss of a child while still caring for your other child. You are caught between two worlds— your thoughts are with your child who died even as you are with your living child.

When your child's sibling died, they were robbed of parts of their past, present, and future. Siblings share a history unique to them, with similar memories, experiences, and connections. They shared fights, inside jokes, loyalty, and competition. The loss of their sibling, their first companion, will always be with them. One teen said, "I wanted my sister to be my maid of honor. We talked about it. We dreamed we would be moms together." Your child will grieve the loss of their sibling for the rest of their life.

Because we work out many of our life skills in our sibling relationships, they often involve conflict and jealousy alongside fierce love and devotion. The complexity of a sibling relationship means there may be regret over what was said or not said. Your child may feel survivor guilt and wonder why it wasn't them who died.

Children often wonder if they will contract a similar illness as their sibling, or they develop fears about how their sibling died if it was an accident. The world they once thought was safe now feels frightening, and they may fear others will die or get sick and may worry about your safety as their parent.

Your assurance of their safety and how you care for yourself can help assuage some of their fears. Affirm your child's concerns by thanking them for telling you how they feel. Acknowledge their fears and share your own: "I feel afraid sometimes too." Let them know you are there for them, for all their feelings and any questions they may have. Ask what helps them feel calm when they're worried and look for solutions together. Offer physical activities like asking to see how high they can jump, kneading clay together, or blowing bubbles outside. Invite older children and teens to take a walk with you in nature. Provide them with a journal and art supplies. Ask them to find or create a playlist that matches their mood while they write and draw.

Healing Through Your Unimaginable

As you reel from all that has been taken from your future and your family, you may not, at this moment, have the capacity to believe in a good that is yet to be. You will carry your child with you and miss them for the rest of your life. You will always wonder what they would be doing or who they would be. There are no magic words for healing. Just a promise that you are healing and will continue to heal from the unimaginable.

Hand over heart, dear reader.
Deep breath in. Let it out. Say aloud,
"I bring compassion to myself in my healing."

HEALING PRACTICES

Reflection

1. In your immediate family, what differences have you noticed in how each of you is grieving?
2. What do you need from a friend or your partner right now? Consider sharing your needs with them and asking what they need from you.

Expressive Arts Invitation: Found Poem

Supplies needed: old magazines, construction paper, glue, and pens or pencils

Using magazines or printed articles, rip or cut out words that stand out to you. Don't overthink the words, just tear them out if they catch your attention. After you have several words, make them into a poem that represents your grief by gluing them onto a piece of construction paper. Write your own words between the ripped-out words if you wish.

Discussion Questions with Your Child

1. What words describe your person?
2. What words describe your grief right now?

A Blessing for When Your Heart Keeps Beating

If your heart keeps beating when theirs has stopped
And what you always feared comes true

If you face the unimaginable
The life you would never choose

If dreams vanish
And you wish you could too

If you long and plead
For it to be different
To go back
To the time before

May you find a hand to hold
May they join your protest in the dark
Your one-word refrain
NO! NO! NO!

May they watch you as you finally sleep
And be there when you wake
Whispering, "You are safe. I am here"
May you never hold the unimaginable alone

5

Honoring Your Connection

I woke up before the sun, preparing for the gymnastics of getting out of bed with Cassie on one side and Cody on the other. Turning sideways, I crawled between them and slipped to the floor, quietly closing the door before heading downstairs.

It was one year after Tyler's accident and death, and we were back in Monterey with his parents. Back to the place where the middle-of-the-night phone call hijacked the life we were building.

Gathering my notebook, Bible, and pen, I walked to my car. As I drove to the beach in the dark, I reflected on the past year. On us. On all that he'd missed: Cassie starting kindergarten, the tiny tree we'd brought home for Christmas, Cody learning to ride a bike without his dad running alongside him.

As the sun rose, I wrote Tyler a letter, telling him how we survived our first year. I sprinkled grains of sand in the binding of my Bible on the page of the verse that had carried me through my year: "God is our refuge and strength, an ever-present help in trouble" (Ps. 46:1).

Later that day, the kids and I returned to the beach for tide pool exploring and telling stories about Daddy. We marked the day by eating his favorites, starting with Lucky Charms and ending with rocky road ice cream.

Our grief didn't end, and the next year would prove to be harder in some ways, but we'd made it, breath by breath, through the first year. And I had hope we could do it again.

Breath by breath has become year by year. Every June 20 the kids and I meet at Tyler's favorite burger place. When they ask the name for our order, we all say, "Tyler." We toast him with milkshakes. And we thank God for carrying us through another year.

T he finality of death is not something you can know all at once. You grieve in bits and pieces. As you grieve your loved one's physical presence, it's healthy to continue honoring your connection. As author Frederick Buechner writes,

> When you remember me, it means that you have carried something of who I am with you, that I have left some mark of who I am on who you are. . . . It means that even after I die, you can still see my face and hear my voice and speak to me in your heart.[1]

Your longing to be physically reattached to your loved one keeps you searching for ways to connect. Just like your brain continues your connection to a body part even after an amputation, you notice a subconscious reaching for your loved one and a conscious rereminding that they're gone. Your continual desire to reconnect your dismemberment represents your longing for them to be physically with you again.[2]

Honoring Your Grief Through Mourning

You are doing the work of your mourning by reflecting on the ways you are attached to your person and finding how you want to keep your bonds. Grief educator Alan Wolfelt explains the difference between grief and mourning as internal versus external responses to loss. *Grief* is whatever you think and feel inside about the death—the thoughts and feelings you have after someone dies. *Mourning* is when you express your grief outside of yourself, such as through crying, talking, or journaling. Grief is your feelings. Mourning is action and how you heal.[3] And since you lost a physical connection with your loved one, it makes sense that to heal and to restore your sense of safety, you need to increase your connection to yourself and others.

As you carry your beloved with you, you will relate to them differently over time. You don't need to work to detach from your person with "closure" or "letting go" but rather allow the redefining of your relationship. Even when our loved ones are gone, we can still bond with them.[4] As author Mitch Albom famously wrote in his book *Tuesdays with Morrie*, "Death ends a life, not a relationship."[5] You may wonder what your loved one would think when you're doing something new, and you may find yourself wanting to share the beauty of an experience with them. Simply saying, "You would love this—I wish you were here," tends to your forever bond, bringing your person into the present moment with you. Or a simple whispered "Thank you" or "I'm sorry" to your loved one helps you mourn as you reconcile with unfinished parts of your relationship.

Take Your Time with What Remains

You are missing all of them—their touch, smile, laughter, and scent. A *linking object* is a way to maintain your connection to your person and how you carry their love with you.[6] Such objects include items that belonged to them and gifts you received from them. You may want to keep their favorite sweater, art, tools, watch, or shoes. One mom shared, "I keep my husband's coffee cup on the counter and wear his T-shirt to bed. It helps me feel like I'm starting and ending my day with him."

Deciding what you want to keep or release of your loved one's belongings are decisions you can make in your own way and in your own time. There is no hurry. You may find comfort in smelling or seeing their clothes in the closet. One dad said, "My daughter kept my wife's perfume and will put it on sometimes when she is especially missing her." You may find solace in creating a prominent place in your home for photos and belongings. Or perhaps you wish to share your loved one's items with family and friends. As one mom said, "When I was ready, and after my children and I decided on what we wanted to keep, we invited our family and my husband's friends over to choose something of his. It was sweet to see what was most meaningful to each one. When friends and family wear my husband's shirts, belt buckles, and hats, we remember when he was wearing those items." Whatever you do is the right choice for you. There is no perfect way.

If your child died, their room may be a sacred space for you to feel close to them. You may want to keep it the same and have a place where their belongings are on display. Or you may find seeing their empty room is too hard. One mom shared, "I didn't like that my son's room was empty. When we got a new puppy after he died, I put the kennel in there and placed plants and lamps in the space to brighten the corners. It helped me feel like there was new life in his room."

If you feel a sudden urge to discard your loved one's belongings, ask a friend or family member to help. Perhaps they can hold them for a time or help you find a place to store them, since you can't know what you or your child will want in the future. Revisiting your choices allows you to make gradual decisions as they feel right for you. One mom whose husband died when her children were young shared, "I kept his belongings over the years, revisiting the sorting of them as time passed. When my children grew older, we decided together what we wanted to keep and what we wished to give away."

For Those with Few Memories

If your child was young when their loved one died, they may have few memories of them or none at all. Other circumstances may affect their ability to remember them, such as relational separation or when your child doesn't have a memory of their sibling because of pregnancy loss or stillbirth. You can support your child by sharing photos, linking objects, and your own memories of your loved one, including memories of times your child had with them when they were young. Ask your family and friends to share stories of your loved one with your child. One mom whose husband died when their daughter was one asked her family and friends to write her daughter letters that reminisced about their times with her dad. She added, "Even though my daughter has no memories of her dad, she has a box full of stories."

Supporting Your Child

As your child develops and grows, their connection with the person who died will change. Explore with your child how they wish to continue their ties with your loved one. Rituals such as visiting places where you feel close to your loved one, sharing memories, and noticing when they "show up" for you honor your connection. One mom noted, "The kids and I look for hearts in nature that remind us of my husband's love for us. We find them in the clouds, rocks, shells, and leaves. When we see them, we say, 'There's Daddy!'"

Your child may hesitate to talk about the person if they think it will make you sad. It's common in a family to play the "protection game" and not talk about the person as a way of shielding each other. Tell your child, "Anytime you want to talk about your dad, I am here. Don't worry that you will make me sad. I like hearing about him." Going against the urge to talk about your loved one disrupts your healthy connection.[7] Speaking about the person won't make you or your child feel worse.

Finding Your Path of Connection

As you talk about your loved one, remember to discuss both the good and the bad. Relationships are complicated, and even the best of them have aspects that frustrate us. When a person dies, there will naturally be parts of them or the life you had together that you miss, and other parts you don't miss. Giving honest attention to the fullness and complexity of your relationship helps you find your most authentic path of connection and honors their humanness and irreplaceability. When you and your child maintain a bond with the person who died, it makes room for the integration of the loss as it affirms your forever relationship. Instead of separation, these connections carry your loved one forward, honoring their significance.

Hand over heart, dear reader. Deep breath in.
Let it out. Say aloud, "May I give myself the
compassion I need as I honor my connection."

HEALING PRACTICES

Honoring Your Connection

Ways to honor your relationship with your loved one:

- Say their name whenever you can in conversations with others and when sharing memories with your child.
- Keep their photo up in your home.
- Make their favorite foods.
- Toast to their memory.
- Visit their favorite restaurant.
- Light a candle in their honor.
- Finish a project they were working on.
- Write them letters.
- Travel to a place you always wanted to visit together.
- Gather with family and friends and share stories.

Reflection

1. What is a linking object you and your child have from your person? What does it mean to you?
2. How can you and your child honor your connection to your loved one? Invite your child to share ideas with you. Share yours with them.

Expressive Arts Invitation: Memory Chain

Supplies needed: colored paper cut into strips, pencils or markers, and a stapler

Have each family member write their favorite memory of your person on a strip of paper. Staple them to each other to create a memory chain.

Expressive Arts Invitation: Rhythmic Expression

- Together with your child, using a drum, piano, or a household object like a wooden spoon and pot, take turns recreating the sound of your person's laughter. Perhaps the sound begins softly and gets louder or is booming from the start. Take turns playing and reflecting the rhythm and sound of your person's laugh, their voice, and some of the phrases you remember them saying.

- Reference a feelings wheel to find the emotion that best suits you now (see the Further Resources section for an example). Take turns playing a rhythm that describes how you feel at this moment. After one person plays a sound, the others can reflect the sound to validate how the person playing the sound is feeling.

Discussion Questions with Your Child

1. What made your person laugh?
2. What part of your person also lives in you? Their sense of humor? Their athletic abilities? Their compassion?

A Blessing for Empty Spaces

For empty wombs and empty rooms
And how they left you way too soon
Mercy

For vacant closets and unmade beds
Fading smells and hats from their head
For sheets that must one day be washed
And laundry baskets with dirty socks

May you be held in what sustains
And may the vibrance of their life remain

For the day you say, "It is time"
And rifle through their quarters and dimes

In what to keep and what to give
And what to hold and how to live

For all the ways their presence stays
And all the ways they slip away
Mercy

6

Finding Your Community

Our small-town community showed up for the kids and me after Tyler died. Sometimes they knew exactly what I needed. One day, when our doorbell rang, I opened the door and my neighbor stood on my porch, holding packages of toilet paper. She said, "I have no words and no idea what to do, but you have a lot of people here, so I thought you might need this."

One friend stopped by almost every day for nine months. She was with me in the mundane: doing paperwork for our family business, taking the kids to school, folding laundry. I felt her physically holding life with me, somehow making it less heavy.

Sometimes I would feel a deep fragility, like I would crumble if someone gave me a little shove. But then I'd feel an unburdening and wonder if someone held us in prayer. One day a friend said, "I am asking God to give me some of your pain." My loss wasn't just mine—it spread far and wide, each person carrying a small piece. I held on to a verse in the Bible about how God comforts us in our troubles so we can support others with the comfort we receive from him (see 2 Cor. 1:3–4).

I felt both alone and not alone. My grief was mine to hold, yet I was experiencing a new kind of love—being held by my community. And I

was taking part in a collective experience of pain that birthed me into a
circle of others who had experienced a loss like mine.

Support and compassion from others planted seeds of new life in
me. And now I witness families caring for each other at Jessica's House.
The encircling of love, tending to our deepest wounds.

J ust like a young child thrives when their needs are met by their caregivers, your loss calls you to share your newfound needs for healing. When you communicate your needs with others, you create opportunities for them to inch closer and steady you.

Feeling Held by Others

When your suffering in grief isn't met with mirroring and compassion, it can register as mental pain. Mirroring is when someone reflects your facial expression and body language back to you through empathy, showing they want to connect. Feeling dismissed or being met with silent indifference increases your distress. The wildness of your grief needs to be expressed the way it is felt. And it needs to be witnessed and held by those who won't fall away when faced with the intensity of your honest expression.

You may be surprised as some people you thought would be your biggest supporters aren't there for you as you hoped. Perhaps they don't have the capacity, or they aren't the right match for the fragility of your sorrow. One mom said, "Some of my closest friends didn't know how to meet me in my grief, but a neighbor I barely knew, who had a similar loss, showed up when I needed her most." Sadly, some might add even more pain to your shattered heart, and others could be neutral—neither helping nor hurting. Not everyone knows how to be there for someone who is grieving. One bereaved dad shared that one of his friends said, "I'm sorry I stopped talking to you. Your loss was just too much for me," leaving him feeling more alone.

Some friends or family members could surprise you with how well they come alongside you. You may discover your supporters have strengths that are new to you. One person may be a good listener, and another may offer practical support. Additionally, your grief needs change over time. Some supporters are good in the early days, and others are better as steady, long-term helpers.

Changes in Community

You are living with your loss in connection with others and finding ways to grieve together with different personalities, grief reactions, and dynamics with family and friends. Your relationships impact the landscape of your grief. Misunderstandings happen after a loss since each person affected in your circle will experience grief differently. Your emotions are high, and your coping skills are tapped. Each person wants to have their loss validated and acknowledged in the way they are experiencing it. It's common to want to compare pain, even when you are grieving the same loss.

You may notice that your most intimate relationships with your parents, in-laws, children, extended family with aunts, uncles, and cousins, and friends have changed. *You* have changed, and each person affected by the loss has changed. Because death often makes people feel uncomfortable, interactions can be awkward, leaving you feeling like you did something wrong. You are learning to live with others in unfamiliar ways. As one dad said, "I don't call it my 'new normal.' I call it my 'not normal.'"

Shifts in relationships can add to your grief. Any previous tension may intensify. When you are living in the fragility of grief, comments that were once viewed as harmless may feel offensive. One mom said, "I had a falling out with my in-laws after the death of my husband. The conflict left my daughter grieving not only for her dad but also for her grandparents." Conversely, sometimes current conflicts are put aside early in grief because what once seemed important doesn't matter as much. In her book *Never the Same*, grief advocate and educator Donna Schuurman writes,

> The loss of one family member leaves a gap resulting in a loss of equilibrium for the entire family, like removing one piece of a mobile unbalances the whole thing. This [loss] can change not only your daily routines, but the very fabric of how the family members relate to each other.[1]

How to Be Companioned

When you feel securely connected to those you trust, you know you aren't alone. Someone else is carrying your loss with you. The word *compassion* means "suffer with." As you find those who will suffer with you, teach them what you need. Or you may not know what you need right now, but perhaps you know what you *don't* need. Your supporter's role is not to find solutions but to be with you in the ways you find most healing. Like every human, you have a deep need to belong. Because loss often compromises your sense of belonging, you need ongoing, attuned relationships.

You can teach your friends and family how to care for you by communicating your needs. One mom said, "I wrote on my social media, 'When you see me, just give me a hug and say you love me.' It really helped with those awkward encounters." One dad said he learned to say, "That's true, but not helpful," when words or attempts of support from others were more harmful than beneficial. Another mom shared that she liked it when her friends reminded her of fun memories of her partner. She added, "I love it when we watch silly videos and engage in dark humor. Laughter sees me through some of my saddest days, sharing the fun and hard moments with my friends."

There could be times when support is offered but you aren't in a place to receive it. If you don't have the capacity to respond to texts or calls, try saying, "I see your calls and texts but don't have the energy to respond. It helps to know you're there." One mom said her best friend called her every night for six months after her son died. She added, "Even though I didn't always answer, I felt comforted by her call." Engage with your supporters at the pace that feels right for you.

When your community helps you, you might feel a sense of indebtedness. One dad said that after his wife died, a neighbor stopped him to ask if he liked the meal she dropped off. He went on, "I didn't even remember the meal. And I felt annoyed that she would even ask and expect an acknowledgment." Know that when you're grieving, there is no traditional thank-you card or reciprocity required. If you want to express gratitude, there is no timeline. You can write or say thank you if it feels like a natural expression of appreciation and not an obligation. Aligning your actions with your heart is your most healing path.

How to Handle the "How Are You" Question

Our culture's greeting asks the question, "How are you?" You may find it difficult to know how to respond to such a weighty question. How can you stay true to yourself and still feel safe in answering?

First, do a quick check-in with yourself. Are you emotionally up to answering honestly? Or do you feel like giving a short answer? Next, think about the person who is asking. Are they looking for a partial answer? Or will they hold your response and feelings in the way you need? One mom shared, "I began asking them what answer they were looking for by saying, 'Do you want my quick answer? Or the truth?' The number of people who said they wanted to hear the truth surprised me and gave me permission to be honest."

The trouble with "How are you?" is that the intention of the question may differ depending on the person asking it. They may truly want to know and be ready to listen as you share. But this phrase can also be a simple greeting. When you're grieving, it can be a painful one. As one mom commented, "I remind myself they're not asking me about my loss, they're simply saying 'hello.'" One dad said he feels annoyed when asked how he's doing, adding, "What I really want to do is yell, 'How do you think I'm doing?' I try to remind myself that people don't know what to say." As one teen said, "When my mom asks how I'm doing, she really wants to know. I appreciate when she tunes out distractions and truly listens to me." Others may ask, "How are you?" but deliver the question in a pitying tone. One teen voiced, "It feels like pity when they change their tone of voice and lean their head to one side."

While some encounters may call for short responses, providing vague answers can also leave you feeling disconnected. As you learn who you can be honest with and practice genuinely expressing yourself, you create opportunities for connection. Having "back pocket" responses can help you guide the conversation. As one mom said, "Early in my grief, my answer was, 'I'm functional but sad.' Now my response is, 'Okay . . . grading on a curve,' or maybe 'Hanging in there.' If I don't feel up to answering honestly, I say, 'Okay,' then change the subject." Another dad said that his go-to response is, "Thank you for asking. It's hard, but we're doing okay."

Platitudes

Platitudes are thoughtless clichés spoken in the hopes of soothing discomfort. While the sentiment may come from genuine intention, platitudes offered to someone who is grieving can feel like false comfort. Any sentence that begins with "At least" is a platitude. Minimizing statements like, "At least they're not in pain anymore," or "You are so strong," dismiss the enormity of your loss. As one mom mentioned, "When people tell me, 'You're so strong,' I feel like I need to hold myself up to that standard the next time I see them. And most of the time I don't feel strong."

Being the recipient of these ill-fitting statements may leave you feeling angry. As one mom put it, "After the death of my daughter, someone told me, 'Everything happens for a reason,' to which I wanted to respond, 'Please share the reason you think my daughter isn't here with me.'" Another dad said, "After my son died, a few people said, 'It must have been God's plan.' I started responding, 'Well, it wasn't in my plan to not have my child here with me.'"

Just as with the "How are you?" question, it can help to have responses ready for the next time you receive a platitude. If someone says, "You are so strong," you could respond, "It may look that way, but I'm actually having a really hard time." If they say, "They are in a better place," you could respond, "That doesn't feel true because I want them here with me." If they say, "They wouldn't want you to be sad," you could respond, "My sadness reflects my love for them." If they say, "Time heals all wounds," you could respond, "I'm going to love them forever, so I'm going to miss them forever."

You may notice you also offer platitudes to yourself. There's a difference between intentionally choosing to switch your mindset, such as, *I can hold this feeling and make it to my next moment*, and dismissing your own feelings by telling yourself, *I'm stronger than this; I should be able to manage*. If you find you are giving yourself unkind or buck-up messages or holding on to similar messages from others, try breathing in compassion. Bring your hands over your heart as you inhale and say to yourself, *It's understandable that I feel this way*. Then exhale as you push your hands away as if moving the messages that don't support your healing away from you. Repeat until you feel a shift in your breathing pattern and are naturally taking deeper breaths.

Time Alone and with Others

Whether you lean toward introversion or extroversion, it's necessary to have both time alone and time with others who support you. If you are an introvert, you might need solitude to write your thoughts or reflect on your internal experience with your loss. For extroverts, processing with friends and family and having people around can help stabilize your emotions and help you find what you need. One dad said, "After our son died, I needed my friends around me. We talked late into the night around a firepit outside our home. But my wife needed time alone. We learned to respect each other's differences."

As you discover your ideal ratio of solitude and companionship, know that you will have an ongoing need for both. If you find you are avoiding your grief through constant social interactions, it could be time to retreat to do your inner work. As you retreat, gather resources that will nurture you, like a journal, a favorite snack, a candle, or a book to read. And if you are spending a lot of time alone, try being with others. The balancing of your emotions through coregulation, where one person's nervous system calms another's, can help stabilize your mood, even when in a public place like a coffee shop, park, or library. Your restoration path is through both healthy engagement and retreating. Engage. Retreat. Repeat.

Supporting Your Child

Some children can feel isolated when their peers don't understand their loss. Give your child language to use when their peers say words that aren't helpful or are even hurtful. One child said that one of her friends from school told her that she understood how she felt because her cat died, to which the child replied, "A cat's not the same as my dad." After her dad died, another child said a fellow student questioned why she laughed. She replied, "I'm still the same person. I'm sad about my dad sometimes, but I still like to laugh and have fun."

Your teenager might be surprised at who is and is not there for them, leaving them confused about their friendships. Some friends may want to be closer to your teen right after the death but then disappear. Others might surprise them with their presence. After the death of his dad, one teen described the comfort he felt from visitors who came over every day for a week to remember his dad's life and pray the rosary. When asked what they did to provide comfort, he responded, "They showed up." Assure your teen that changes in friendships are common after loss and that there is nothing they did to cause a shift in their relationships.

Your Home Team

How do you find the companions most helpful to you? Consider who you want on your home team. You may have a wide circle of support, but not everyone is helpful. Identify the roles of those who can support you in different ways. Who is empathetic? Who can be with you in your anger? Who can take daily walks with you? Who can give you a hand with household tasks? Who do you trust to help with your kids? Who can you call regardless of the time of day or night? One mom whose husband died said, "One night, I woke up with a wicked bout of a stomach virus. I was sick alone for the first time. My husband had always checked on me as I laid on the bathroom floor. I called the friend I knew would answer. She stayed on the phone with me through the night and invited the kids and me over the next day. She made a bed for me, played a movie, and kept me hydrated while my kids played with hers."

Maybe you feel your home team is lacking. You don't have the capacity to nurture new relationships, activities, or hobbies you once did. Shortly after moving to a new town, one mom's husband died while she was still establishing her community. She said, "I spent a lot of time connecting via video calls with my family and friends back home and joined an online group of bereaved moms."

Over time you may discover a newfound capacity to find new routines alone or with others, learn something new, or rekindle a fondness for a hobby you once enjoyed. You may find you want to be with others who have faced a similar loss. One mom said, "When I finally connected with other moms who had lost a child, it felt like they had a passport to my heart no one else had." Community-based and online support groups are good places to find those who understand what it's like to experience a loss like yours.

Remember that any heavy work becomes lighter when you hold it with others. Having a community, no matter how small, to hold your pain will help you move toward healing.

Hand over heart, dear reader. Deep breath in.
Let it out. Say aloud, "May I find the support
I need as I discover my community."

HEALING PRACTICES

Reflection

Who Are My People?

Together with your child, reflect on your community as well as your needs.

I can share my memories of the person who died with _____ .
_____ makes me laugh.
I feel comfortable crying with _____ .
I can call _____ when I need to talk.
When I want to have fun, _____ is the best person.
_____ understands when I just want to be alone and will give me my space.
I feel safest when I'm with _____ .

What Do I Need?

Together with your child, reflect on who is helpful or unhelpful during this season. Write out what you need from them.

When I'm sad, it helps when you _____ .
When I'm overwhelmed, it helps when you _____
_____ .
When we are together, please _____ .
A helpful activity for me is _____ .
The household chores I need help with the most are _____
_____ .
It helps when you _____ .

Expressive Arts Invitation: My Survival Tree

Supplies needed: paper and markers or colored pencils

Together with your child, draw a tree, including:

Roots: What brings you strength?

Ground: Who supports you?

Trunk: What are your strengths?

Branches: What are your hopes and dreams?

Leaves: Who cares for you?

Weather: What storms are you facing?

Tree Pose

Modify according to your and your child's age and ability.

- Feel your feet on the floor. Think about what brings you strength and keeps you rooted.
- Place your weight on your right foot. What are the storms that make you feel off balance? What steadies you? Keep your focus forward and think about a person who cares for you. Keep your right leg straight without locking your knee.
- Bend your left leg and bring the sole of your left foot onto your right leg either on your inner calf or inner thigh, not your inner knee.
- Focus your gaze on something that doesn't move. Think about your roots and what helps steady you in a storm.
- Try raising your hands to the sky. Imagine reaching for those who love you.
- Take three breaths, lower your hands and then your left foot, and try the other side.

Discussion Questions with Your Child

1. What helps you feel strong?
2. How have you grown since your person died?

A Blessing in What Remains

In their absence, may you find presence
May your splintered heart be held
May your holes become wholeness
And your emptiness be touched by hands of love

When your days are filled with open spaces
May your longing heart be another's calling

May they find you in the dark
And hold you in their care
Tuck you in
Sing you to sleep

May their song be your refrain
Until you find your voice
In what remains

7

Grief and Belief

At Carter's graveside service, I wanted to break the windows in the hearse that held him. I screamed, "No!" and gave full vent to my protest that God allowed my son to die.

In the months that followed, I opened myself to a raw process of grief I had not allowed with other deaths in my life.

I had always trusted God's will. When Tyler died, I thought if two planes collided on a beautiful June day, it must be part of a greater plan. For some reason, I didn't ask why. On Tyler's grave marker, I wrote, "In His Will Is Our Peace."

But after Carter died, I screamed "No!" at God most mornings and decided he wasn't safe or good.

My world felt dangerous. I wondered if life was reduced to physics and my prayers for safety didn't matter. I thought of the way Carter's car slipped on the road and how it crashed in just the right place for his head to hit a tree.

Did God look away? I thought he was watching over us, but now I felt like an open target for annihilation.

Even though I was raised as an atheist, I had always felt God's love and presence, even when I was a child. But Carter's death shattered my trust.

I wanted there to be some kind of shelter. To know I was held by hands of love.

One morning, about a year and a half after Carter's death, I sensed a gentle presence of love and comfort pressing in: I will renew your trust in me because it comes from me.

It takes as long as it takes.

I f faith is part of your life, you may notice it beginning to reshape after the death of your loved one. During these unsettling times, you may find comfort in God and draw strength from your relationship with him. Or perhaps God has never felt so distant to you.

Your faith community might be a deep source of comfort, with their support bringing you strength during this time. Perhaps the rhythms of spiritual practices and communal gatherings provide a rich sense of connection with God and those around you. Some parents share that their church helped them through their darkest days after their loved one died.

Or questions like, *Why did God allow this to happen?* could scream within you. You might be doubting your safety in the world and wondering how what happened to you could pass through God's hands.

Healing Within Your Faith

You could be experiencing a newfound strength and peace you've never known quite like this. Signs that God is holding you through the unimaginable may be tangible, and you may notice how God is showing up for you in the ways you need. One mom said, "I felt God meeting me moment by moment: a text from a friend, a feeling of comfort, arms to welcome me when I needed them most. It reminded me of a verse in the Bible that says, 'I see your love and tender care everywhere'" (Ps. 119:64 TPT). Another mom voiced,

"I looked for God's mercies that he promised were new every morning. Somehow, God's faithfulness sustained me through my darkest nights. When I held a warm cup of coffee in my hand in the morning, I felt his divine love and provision helping me to face my day."

You may find comfort in your belief that you will see your loved one again someday. One mom commented, "A deep sense of peace surprised me after my husband died. I felt surrounded by a warm bubble and buoyed by a sense of comfort beyond my understanding. While praying one day, I felt a deep sense of calm and wondered if that's what my husband felt in heaven."

Part of grief is to question what is beyond your comprehension. Loss invites you to reexamine your beliefs and reflect on your mortality. It's natural for you to want to make sense of the senseless. You might wonder, *Is there a heaven?* or *Will I really see them again someday?* Your child could be asking similar questions. When you admit your questions to them, it normalizes their feelings and lessens shame. Listening to their wonderings creates a safe place for them to sift their thoughts.

You could be met with well-intentioned sentiments from others in your faith community. One mom said she prayed for her daughter to get well, and God didn't answer as she hoped. After her daughter died, others tried to comfort her by saying, "She's in a better place." She learned to respond with, "I would give anything to have her here with me." As another mom put it, "I prayed all my son's life that he would know God and be in heaven someday. I just realized my prayers were answered. Not how I hoped, but my son is safe." Another mom shared, "At first, I was angry at God, and then I felt betrayed. I drifted alone for a time, wondering if the world would ever make sense again."

Premature Healing

In faith communities, the idea of an afterlife can force grievers into premature hope. However, the truth is you can delight in the belief that your loved one is safe in heaven and at the same time deeply grieve the loss of their physical presence in your life. The sacred work of honoring your grief means you don't minimize your heartache. Your nervous system is overwhelmed when you neglect to align with your suffering, leading to a more complicated grief process.

In times past when someone died, sacred rituals helped those in mourning connect with their faith. Family members took part in bathing and dressing the body after death. Friends and family gathered, spent time with the body, and grieved together. Grievers outwardly showed they were mourning by not grooming or by wearing clothes that signaled their time of bereavement. When we abide by society's expectation to hurry through our time of mourning or don't have clothing or traditions that set us apart, we miss the healing benefits of these practices.

Perhaps you've heard the famous story behind the hymn "It Is Well with My Soul." Its composer, Horatio Spafford, sent his wife, Anna, to Europe on a ship with their four daughters. During a storm, their daughters died when their ship collided with another and sank. As the story goes, Anna sent a message to her husband that said, "Saved alone." When Horatio traveled to meet her, he sailed by the accident site, and there he penned the words to the hymn.[1] We don't know the anguish Horatio went through to write those words or the full account of what really happened. Yet the story of this hymn has been told in faith communities as an example of how to grieve when you lose everything.

The Bible gives accounts of honest expression. The psalmist said, "My soul is in deep anguish" (Ps. 6:3). In torment, Jesus asked his Father, "Why have you forsaken me?" (Matt. 27:46). Even in creation, darkness comes before light. Maybe Job, who lost all his children, screamed this verse: "Therefore I will not restrain my mouth; I will speak in the anguish of my spirit; I will complain in the bitterness of my soul" (Job 7:11 ESV). He didn't hold back his feelings of betrayal. "For he crushes me with a tempest and multiplies my wounds without cause; he will not let me get my breath, but fills me with bitterness" (9:17–18 ESV).

Because grief is a reaction to loss, we will feel pain. Our faith doesn't cancel our suffering. One dad mentioned someone said to him, "Those who believe need not grieve." This platitude left him feeling like if he grieved, he *didn't* believe. Questioning God and aching for your loved one, even if you trust they are in heaven, doesn't mean you have lost your faith. Holding opposites of faith and fear, belief and unbelief, trust and doubt, means you are human.

Supporting Your Child

Your child may also be questioning their faith. Their honest process is an opportunity for you to lean into their newfound place of wrestling with what once may have felt uncomplicated before the death. They may wonder, "Does God care?" or "Can I trust God?" One dad shared how his teen son questioned his faith after the death of his sibling, adding, "I found I didn't have answers to his questions. So, I learned to listen and question with him." Your child may find comfort in trusting their loved one is safe in heaven and at the same time feel angry at God that they are physically separated from them.

You may find that exploring your child's questions, tangled emotions, and doubts is difficult for you. Examining your beliefs can be a natural part of grief and an opportunity for your child to reflect on their sources of hope and strength. Their time of questioning builds fortitude for what they may face in their future, helping them to find what helps them through seasons of loss and change.

Wherever You Are Is Just Right

You might find other ways to nurture your spirituality and find being in nature helps you feel connected to the rhythms of life and death. Perhaps practices like meditation and yoga draw you. One mom who didn't attach to a specific set of beliefs found comfort in her pet: "After my husband died at the hospital, I returned home alone. I could tell our dog sensed something wrong when I walked through the door. I lay on my bed, and our dog, who usually slept in the other room, leaped onto the bed, placed his head on my chest, and kept it there through the night." Some have found comfort in noticing signs they believe were sent from their loved one: a butterfly, a hummingbird, an animal in the wild like a fox, or a vibrant sunset. One mom said, "One time, as I sat next to my son's grave, a large white owl landed in a tree by me. I felt my son's presence. It was like he said, 'I'm okay, Mom.'"

You may find yourself in a different place than others in your family. After the death of their daughter, one mom said she struggled with her faith while her husband relied on his more than ever. She added, "Going to church was a source of strength for him, while I found it way too hard. The worship didn't reflect my sentiments at the time, and seeing my friends' intact families sitting together was just too painful. We both learned to respect the other's choice in doing what felt right at the time." One husband said, "I admired my wife's trust and dependence on God after our son died. For me, God felt so far away. So I borrowed a little bit of her faith until I found my own again."

If you find yourself grappling with the spiritual wound of loss and your most profound questions of faith, permit yourself to be in the process of deepening trust or doubt. Perhaps your beliefs strengthen you when you need God the most. Or perhaps you need to be with your fury at the injustice that God allowed your loss. Allow yourself to explore your anger, skepticism, trust, and hope. Your honest reflection makes room for what you need.

Hand over heart, dear reader. Deep breath in.
Let it out. Say aloud, "I give myself the compassion
I need as I welcome my sacred wonderings."

HEALING PRACTICES

Reflection

1. Where are you with your faith right now?
2. What is an answer you wish you had?

Expressive Arts Invitation: A Letter to God

Supplies needed: pen and paper

Using the two reflection questions above, write a letter to God or a letter from God to you. In your writing, ask your most profound questions.

If faith is not part of your life, write a journal entry on what in the natural world helps you feel connected and anchored. How has the world failed you or held you?

Expressive Arts Invitation: Kneading Your Emotions

Supplies needed: modeling clay

Together with your child, notice the clay's texture, earthlike smell, and coolness in your hands.

Punch, knead, or throw it down on a solid surface, paying attention to how it sounds.

Work it into a shape that reflects your questions. Express your response to the shattering of your hopes and dreams as you knead it.

End your time by using the "lion's breath." Breathe in for four seconds, hold for four seconds, then breathe out in a roar for eight seconds. Notice the difference you feel in your body when you are done.

Discussion Questions with Your Child

1. What did the smell of the clay remind you of?
2. What sound did the clay make when it hit the table?
3. How did your hands and arms feel when you were done kneading the clay?
4. How did your body feel after you roared?

A Blessing in the Doubt

When your faith shifts to unbelief
When you wonder
Was the one who was once your refuge looking away?
Did he not notice?
Did he turn his face when you needed him most?

When you wake up and remember
What you feared
It happened

How did it happen?
How could God let it happen?
To you? To them? To us?

When your foundation crumbles
When you are left with the emptiness
The absence of your beloved

May what comes in the torn apart places
Be the dust that swirls into form
To join you in what remains

To lean in with a whisper
With a stubborn "I am here"
To bind you to the One who sees

8

The Weather of Your Grief

One late December night I drove with my dog, Douglas, to a neighboring town to get my favorite hot cocoa. After Carter died, I found comfort in drinking hot cocoa every night before bed. It was raining and dark, and as I made my way there, I decided to take the back roads home to avoid the freeway during the storm.

But then I remembered—the back way was where Carter's accident had happened. Our family had visited the site after the accident, but we didn't drive on the curve where he lost control. Before his accident, in all the years driving that road, I'd never noticed the curve.

Douglas sat up and looked sideways at me from the passenger seat as I drove around the slight curve in the rain. I yelled, "This is the curve, Carter? This? You should have made it home!"

Carter had been our most cautious kid. He never had stitches or broken bones. Our only emergency room visit was when he stuck a raisin up his nose as a toddler.

Why did he drive so fast that night? Was there anything I could have done to stop him? I tried to think of all the ways.

One early foggy morning, about a year after his accident, panic surprised me as I drove into a lane with construction barriers on both sides. I wondered if it was related to Carter's accident. With large trucks in front of and behind me, I catastrophized with thoughts of an accident.

Later I worked with my counselor, who guided me to deepening practices of finding calm in my body while driving. I learned to use bilateral movements, alternating squeezing my hands on the steering wheel and using my voice with a "voo" sound to simulate natural vibration and quiet the overactivity of my nervous system. I imagined pushing the walls away with my hands. Using these tools led to feelings of calm and safety. They gave me the confidence to remember my body is a resource whenever I face a perceived threat.

There were other times I felt shut down. I didn't cry at Carter's funeral. A feeling of numbness settled over me in the too-muchness of the gathering. I wanted everyone to know Carter like I did. But how could I put his life into a two-hour memorial service? What pictures do you choose? What stories do you tell? What songs do you sing?

I'd spent twenty-five years planning other people's funerals and supporting their families, but I felt lost on how to honor Carter's life in the way he deserved. Nothing I said or did could ever be enough.

And I was just too sad to cry.

There are still times when nothing feels good or right. And I live with a sense of homesickness—I want to go home. But it's gone.

Y ou may notice that the rhythms of your grief follow a similar cadence to other parts of the natural world, like the weather. Just as with a heat wave or a cold front, there is brewing, peaking, and receding. The energy of grief in your body, especially if you experienced a loss with trauma, affects your inner climate. Grief is an external force that stirs up internal responses. Your bodily sensations move your weather vane and point you to the resources you need. You may need rest, the calming presence of one of your supporters, a quiet room, or to physically move.

80

Finding Your Just-Right Place

If you notice sensations like panic, anxiety, or rage, you may be experiencing a "heat wave." Or you may feel shut down, numb, or empty, which is a "cold front." There's a window in the middle where you'll find your "just-right" place, or ideal climate. UCLA professor Dan Siegel calls this ideal climate our "window of tolerance" in his book *The Developing Mind*, explaining that each person has a range in the intensity of emotions within which they can experience, process, and integrate.[1] Here, you can hold and express your emotions without becoming overwhelmed.

When you are grieving, and especially when your grief is accompanied by an experience where you lacked the resources you needed for safety, both real and perceived threats can push you out of your ideal climate. Threats include anything that reminds you of the person's death or makes you feel unsafe and powerless. You could be activated by a smell, a sound, a similar story to yours, or even the cast of light at sunset, signaling night's approaching darkness.

Everyone's window of tolerance is different. How long do you feel comfortable being in weather that is too windy, too wet, too hot, or too cold? The warmth of the sun can feel good. But after a long period of time or at a temperature that is too high, it may become uncomfortable or even unbearable. The same holds true for being out in a rainstorm. Just as everyone has a different tolerance for rain or heat, everyone has a different just-right place emotionally where they are calm, alert, and engaged.

Finding Your Resources

You can stay in the rain longer if you are wearing a raincoat. Even longer if you are also holding an umbrella. "Weather gear," or resources, will help you to be outside your window of tolerance for longer periods and expand your capacity.[2]

One dad whose wife died in the hospital found his resource: "I had a lot of anxiety if I had to take the kids to the doctor for their check-up or visit someone in the hospital. It helped to bring a family member for support." With the change of seasons, our bodies must learn to acclimate to new temperatures. Similarly, looking at the "forecast" when assessing threats to your sense of safety can help you find the resources needed to face what's ahead. The expansion of your window is how you acclimate.[3] You will always have a limit in your capacity. And, at times, you may need to retreat "indoors," back to your ideal climate. Start by going to the edges of your discomfort and back to your safe place. Attuning to your body in small ways helps you find what you need. How tired are you? Are you hungry? Thirsty?

Think of a time when you felt your most secure, nonjudgmental, and openhearted. What did you notice about your heartbeat? The rhythm of your breath? How did the muscles in your neck feel? Reflecting on when you have felt fully alive and engaged can help you remember what you need. Notice when your need for sensory safety is met, your heartbeat is steady, and your breathing and muscles are relaxed. Your just-right place is where you feel flexible, supported, curious, emotionally regulated, and connected to others and yourself.[4]

Coregulation is when you benefit from being with someone who is in their ideal climate. Their calming presence attunes to your needs in an empathetic and supportive way. When a friend is in their own window of tolerance, it helps regulate your nervous system because your brain is wired with mirror neurons that help you match others' emotional states. Physician and trauma researcher Gabor Maté says, "We can't fix what can't be fixed, but we can be the witness who supports the healing capacity we all hold within."[5]

During a Heat Wave

When you're in a "heat wave," remember that your body is a resource. Simply slowing down your breathing can help in the moment.

Try self-soothing touch, like pressing your hands over your heart while giving yourself kind messages from a loving parent: "You are safe." When your out-breath is longer than your in-breath, your anxiety will lessen as you downregulate, or "cool off." Breathing in for four seconds, holding your breath for seven seconds, and then breathing out for eight seconds is a proven way to slow your heart rate and lower your blood pressure, bringing you back to your ideal climate.[6]

Other ways to bring yourself back into your just-right place are by swaying from side to side, humming, rubbing your hands together and placing them over your eyes, practicing yoga, wrapping your arms around yourself with alternate tapping on the sides of your arms, immersing your hands or body in warm water, or moving to music.

During a Cold Front

A "cold front" can leave you feeling shut down, with little energy or motivation. When you "freeze," your brain shuts down as a protective response when your nervous system is overloaded. Your brain is good at keeping you safe by numbing during times of distress, but over time this can impact your emotional well-being. You might find it's hard to get out of bed, realize you are isolating yourself from activities and people, notice your body feels heavy, or find that talking takes too much effort. Although grief has a way of slowing you down, if you are feeling *shut down*, bring gentle awareness to what you need. If you want to inch closer to your sweet spot of engagement, energy, and curiosity, try drinking or immersing your hands in cold water, listening to upbeat music, eating something crunchy such as ice or a tangy, chewy candy, pushing against a wall, or lifting something heavy.

Supporting Your Child

Have you ever encountered a severe storm and felt powerless against its forces? You and your child may feel overpowered by your grief reactions. Intense sadness, fear, anger, and confusion capable of overwhelming their mind and body may be new for your child. Depending on their age, they may find it difficult to understand and express their feelings. What you visually see may be different from what is happening under the surface. If you look past behaviors of anger or rage, you will likely find fear or sadness. When trying to understand how your child is feeling, instead of wondering what is wrong, ask yourself, *What is my child showing me about the weather inside of them because of what happened?* Help your child name what they are feeling and normalize common reactions by sharing examples of times you have felt similarly, being mindful not to overburden them. Reflections such as, "I see you're angry. I get mad sometimes too," help them feel understood and give language to what they are experiencing.

As you learn ways to return to your just-right place, your stable and calm presence supports your child through coregulation. When your child's inner climate is stormy, your nervous system mirrors their hormone production and joins them in freeze, flight, or fight mode. If you can regulate *your* nervous system, they can mirror yours instead. You can help calm their storm by changing *your* inner climate. Say to your child, "I'm going to sit down with you and breathe for one minute because it helps me feel better." When you calm yourself first, you can better support your child.

After calming yourself, engage your child in practices to return to *their* sweet spot where they can think, learn, and relax. Try standing with or holding them while taking slow, deep breaths together. While facing them, hold their hands and alternate squeezing one at a time. Together, shake your arms and hands out to your sides. Sway from side to side. If your child doesn't want to engage, you can still model this movement and narrate what you are doing: "Swaying side to side and taking deep breaths helps me feel better." Offering yourself as a container, one capable of holding them and their emotions, teaches them it is possible to bend with the storm, not break.

A Healthy Integration of Your Loss

Just as you will never again experience the weather like it is at this moment, trust that the climate of your grief is always changing. You heal as you go through it, not around it, at a time and pace that feel right for you. Even the sun won't cast the exact same light today in the way it did yesterday. You may morph from fierce winds with pelting rain to a gentle breeze on a sunny day.

Hand over heart, dear reader. Deep breath in.
Let it out. Say aloud, "I bring compassion to myself.
May I trust that a storm never lasts forever."

HEALING PRACTICES

Reflection

1. When do you notice you feel most anxious, angry, or fearful (heat wave)?
2. When do you notice feeling shut down, numb, or disconnected (cold front)?
3. What helps you get back to your just-right place?

Expressive Arts Invitation: Storms of Grief

Supplies needed: paper and markers, crayons, colored pencils, or watercolors

Explain to your child that storms of emotions happen in grief. Identifying emotions helps them find ways to cope. If your grief were a storm, what kind would it be? Rainstorm? Thunderstorm? Tornado? Hurricane? Blizzard? Draw a picture of what your "grief storm" looks like. What helps you come back to your just-right place when you are in your storm? List some ways you can help yourself, such as talking to someone you trust, screaming into a pillow, or taking a walk.

Expressive Arts Invitation: My Weather Gauge

Supplies needed: paper and pencil or colored pencils

On a blank piece of paper, draw a cloud on the left side of the page and a sun on the right side of the page. Draw a line between the sun and the cloud. Have your child mark an "X" to show where they are between the sun and the cloud. Help your child identify what could help them move toward their "ideal climate" in the middle of their gauge.

Discussion Questions with Your Child

1. What does a grief storm feel like in your body?
2. What do you need most when you're in the middle of a grief storm?

A Blessing in the Storm

When the siren sounds
And in your bones you know the storm is coming
May your body be your shelter

May your breath be the wave
That rises and falls
And like the moon pulls the tide
May the wisdom of your body guide you

Lie on the earth
It will not fall away
Let the storm pass over you

And then stand

Notice the strength of your spine
Once again
You are here

Tethered by roots of love

9

Grief in Your Body

The physical sensations I felt after Carter died surprised me. There was an energy in my body that had to be released. Sometimes I found myself groaning out such long sobs that it was hard to inhale. I felt the most primal energy that could only exit through a scream. Other times a tightness in my throat made me feel like something was stuck. One day, after yoga, I sobbed on my mat at the end of class. I didn't want to scare anyone, but my grief was so wild and raw.

Another day I drove to fetch a few items from the store. As I walked through the parking lot, my body felt incredibly heavy, like someone was pressing down on my shoulders. I stood in the aisles, trying to remember why I was there, searching for an answer to my hollowness. I wiped away tears with the fleece of my jacket sleeve as I stood in the checkout line. There was nothing to fill the vacancy of Carter.

Gloom and dread filled me as I drove home. A pressure in my chest made it hard to breathe. Crying always seemed to ease the pain, but now it felt like my tears were wedged in my throat. I scoured my mind for what might bring a sense of relief.

When I walked up to my house, I saw a friend waiting for me at the top of the steps by my front door. As I got closer, she reached out, gently

grasped my shoulders with her hands, and looked into my eyes. Then she
drew me close and held me tight for a long while and witnessed the dark-
ness of my soul. I wept in her arms. She carried the relief I sought as she
aligned with my ache for Carter. She matched my regret; my questions;
my feelings of betrayal, fear of future losses, and anger; my images of the
accident; and my longing wish I could change it all somehow.

A beholding.

T he energy of grief that builds *in* your body must be expressed *through* your body. Think of the word *emotion* as **e** = energy + motion. Emotions need motion. Your body's sensations (as energy) inform your nervous system about how you're doing and what you need. The name you give those sensations points to your feelings. Emotions have a mission: to be felt and expressed. They are there for your healing. Perhaps anger incites you toward change, or sadness connects you with others for comfort.

Emotions Followed by Feelings

Emotions come first, and feelings follow. Emotions are sensations in your body in response to your present experience. Feelings are your personal, internal experience of those emotions and the names you give them. Emotions occur automatically, whereas feelings are based on your perceptions. Past experiences also in-fluence how you relate to your emotions and the feelings with which you identify.

It's common in grief to suppress a feeling before it can accomplish its work of being felt and expressed. Reasoning and interpreting through your cognitive process can interfere with expression. Blink-ing away tears, swallowing the lump in your throat, or distracting yourself through analysis can hinder the opportunity for that feeling to move through you and be experienced and expressed.

You will find what needs to be expressed as energy in your body. Some people describe exhaustion as downward energy, anxiety as spinning, anger as hot and outward, or stress as an energy of pressure inside their bodies. Connecting to the wisdom of your body helps you discern what you need when you're grieving.

Because your brain's job is to respond to signals from your grieving body and keep it in a steady state, it tries to anticipate what you need for survival.[1] When you pay attention to your body's signals, you can find ways to discharge the energy of your grief. Your feelings are there to help you. Fear helps move you to safety, and sadness turns you inward to what is touching you. Longing helps you identify what you want, and anger spurs you to change. Your feelings guide you to your next step.

Your grieving body needs your attention. As you sense your grief in your body, reflect on what you need to keep your flow of expression. Bodies never lie. Perhaps your tiredness demands rest. Regrets may require putting pen to paper and writing everything you wish you could change. Anger often needs expression with large muscles, like lifting something heavy or running. Anxiety can move using your voice or body movement. The act of expression helps prevent the energy of your emotions from getting stuck in your body.

As you process your loss, you may notice you laugh through your tears as you hold opposing energies in grief. You can hold both the darkness and light. A positive marker for mental health is the ability to experience opposite emotions at the same time.[2] Perhaps you've felt guilty when you experience glimmers of relief or happiness alongside your suffering. One dad whose son died said, "When I laugh, I feel the Grief Witch behind me, hitting me over the head with her broom. I feel guilty when I'm having a good moment." Just as it takes a mix of sun and rain to make a rainbow, when we find light in the dark, we experience the richness of beauty and pain within our human experience.

Have you ever noticed how calm you feel after you cry? The act of crying takes what's inside of your body and places it outside.

Author Shauna Niequist writes, "The ability to cry is a sign of health because it means your body and your soul agree on something, and that what your soul is feeling, your body is responding to."[3] The physical showing of tears helps others witness your suffering. Tears contain oxytocin and endorphins. These feel-good chemicals are your nervous system's attempt to ease both physical and emotional pain.[4] Suppressing your tears elevates stress hormones like cortisol, so take the time and space you need to cry.[5]

A Storm Never Lasts Forever

It's natural to feel confused or frightened by the intensity of your grief, and it's understandable if you're worried it will overwhelm you. Once you notice sensations in your body, see if you can stay with the feeling for ninety seconds. As neuroanatomist and stroke survivor Jill Bolte Taylor writes, "When a person has a reaction to something in their environment, there's a 90-second chemical process that happens."[6] Place your hand where you sense the emotion and stay with that feeling as it flows through you. See what's possible. How can your body be a resource to support you through these times? Can you sway from side to side? Suck on a sour candy? Or perhaps someone is nearby who can sit with you in this moment, helping you mirror their calmer state. As you learn to be with what you are sensing, remember that just like the weather, there is a brewing, peaking, and resolving. A storm never lasts forever.

Animals in the wild consistently release traumatic experiences instead of holding and replaying them like humans often do. They find a safe place and allow their bodies to care for them and discharge the "too-muchness" of their experience.[7] Have you ever seen a dog afraid of fireworks who shakes and looks for cover? As humans, if we don't allow our traumatic experiences to flow through us, they can get stuck in our bodies.

How can you discharge a threat from your body? If you experience involuntary shaking, allow it to happen, as this is the way your nervous system releases excess adrenaline and muscle tension, returning you to a neutral state. To mimic involuntary shaking, try doing jumping jacks, stomping your feet, or shaking your body. Even laughter is beneficial as it lowers your stress response by giving your insides a needed shake.

Supporting Your Child

As you sense, name, and express emotions, you align with what is true and expand your sense of safety. As you support your child, remember that when they endure a loss that involves trauma, they may not have words to describe their experience. Aid your child in recognizing the energy of grief in their body and what helps them express it. One child said, "I feel my heart getting heavy like a wet sponge. When I cry, it's like I am squeezing the sponge, and my heart feels lighter."

You can also support your child with physical touch. If they are overwhelmed by worry, your arms wrapped around them in a hug creates a boundary and a container for their experience. Remind them they can physically welcome what helps them and push away what doesn't support them. Together, place your hands at your sides, then bring your hands toward your heart, breathing in what brings you strength. Then forcefully push away your worries with your arms and hands with a loud or whispered roar and long exhale. Repeat until you notice the change needed in your body.

Ask your child to reflect on how their body feels when it finds what it needs. How does their body feel after playing outside? After crying? After talking with someone? After a hug? After eating a food they enjoy? After taking a rest? Awareness of their body helps them access what works for them in times of need.

Moving Your Grief

Bilateral movement engages both sides of your body and helps activate the relaxation response in your brain by helping it form new connections. It connects both sides of the brain, the logic center and the emotion center. When both sides of your brain are engaged, you'll find an increase in both your awareness of how you are doing and your ability to support yourself through it. Depending on your child's age and abilities, some bilateral movement activities to do together may include walking, riding a bike, beating a drum with alternate hands, drawing or painting circles on paper using both hands simultaneously, or giving yourself butterfly hugs—crossing your arms over your chest and rhythmically tapping your hands on your upper arms, alternating right and left. Larger movements might include bopping a balloon back and forth with alternate hands.

Movement helps emotions move through your body. Since about 60 percent of your body is made up of water, it makes sense to keep the flow of movement in your grieving body. When emotions get stuck, you might feel anxiety or a tightness in your throat or shoulders. Invite your child to go on a walk, toss a ball, or throw a Frisbee back and forth to give your worries a break. Clasp your hands together in front of you and open your mouth. Shake your clasped hands and say "Ahh," easing tension in your neck and throat. Scream into a pillow. Get a bowl of ice and take it outside to throw against a hard surface such as a wall, fence, or sidewalk. Notice the sound the ice makes when it hits your target.

Ask your child how they feel after movement compared to before. As they notice differences in their body, it reinforces the feelings of ease that emerge when practicing expression. Attuning to bodily sensations helps children discover what uniquely works for them with their mourning style.

Learning to Trust Your Grieving Body

Notice the cycling of your sensations of grief. How do they mirror nature? Watch the way ocean waves brew, peak, and recede. See the way flowers open at sunrise and close at sunset. Notice the way animals take care of themselves during threats to their safety—the peacock's expansion of tail feathers, the porcupine's quills, the pufferfish doubling its size. These cycles are inside you, too, and your body is a resource, always supporting you to find what you need for safety. Trust your ability to find your way back to feeling at home in your body, again and again.

Hand over heart, dear reader. Deep breath in.
Let it out. Say aloud, "I give myself the compassion
I need as I learn to trust my grieving body."

HEALING PRACTICES

Reflection

Explore these questions with your child so they can become more aware of their emotions. Your child may find it challenging to put words to what they feel. Images make it easier. Try using this check-in to show each other how you are feeling.

1. What happens in your body when you feel overwhelmed? What do you need?
2. What happens in your body when you feel worried? What do you need?
3. What happens in your body when you feel angry? What do you need?
4. What happens in your body when you feel safe? What helps you feel this way? Who helps you feel this way?

Expressive Arts Invitation: Colors of My Heart

Supplies needed: paper and coloring utensils

Together with your child, draw a large heart on a piece of paper and fill it in with all the colors that portray your emotions of grief. You will need a wide spectrum of colors to represent the different and opposing shades of your emotions in grief. As you color, think about what the shades symbolize. For example, yellow could reflect relief, orange disappointment, and red rage. Draw a map key if you wish, showing what emotion each color represents.

Discussion Questions with Your Child

1. What colors of your heart do you want more of?
2. How have the colors of your heart changed since your person died?

A Blessing for Your Body

May your body be your refuge
A holder of discordant notes
Playing the offbeat song
You never wanted to sing

May you notice what brews and swells
And find your way home

Hold a sacred vigil for your proclamation
Will you scream in your car? In the shower?
Punch at the air? Or your pillow?
Will you fall to the floor?
Or dive into the sea?

Give your lament words
Or a form in your body
Assign it a color
Or a shape

Weep it
Breathe it out in silent rage
Utter it in a prayer for mercy

And may you find one to light a candle for your vigil
To honor your sacred expression
To allow your blazing heart
To burn in theirs

10

Expressing Your Grief Through the Arts

A few months after Carter died, my friend and I drove a couple of hours to the beach and arrived right before sunset. We made our way to the top of the wooden beach gate and noticed several women playing drums and tambourines while walking along the shore.

On the twentieth anniversary of Tyler's death, I'd encountered a drum circle at a national conference for children's grief. The conductor invited us to think of a message we wanted to express to the circle and to create a rhythm. My rhythm into the circle sang "Twenty years. I'm alive."

After Carter died, I often felt a profound urge to be part of another healing drum circle. When I saw the women with drums on the beach, I felt like Carter had sent them to me.

We made our way to the sand and kicked off our shoes. When we approached the women, my friend shared that my son had recently died, and I had been hoping for a drum ceremony. One of the ladies gave her hand-painted drum to me and asked for my son's name. They circled me as the sky turned orange and joined in my rhythm as they sang out "CARTER." My unspoken expression in rhythm called "I WILL STAY

ALIVE!" *The beat—Whack. Whack. Whack. Whack-Whack—sent my desire to thrive into the circle, despite my shattered heart.*

I sensed a strong connection to Carter and felt him there with me, surrounded by witnesses of my loss and pain. These beautiful women became our friends. We laughed when we learned we were all from the same hometown!

We never know how healing will show up for us.

E xpressive arts offer a creative outlet for your and your child's emotions, especially those difficult to process consciously. Expressing yourself through art, music, or play helps you and your child regulate and communicate your emotions. Acting out traumatic events through play also provides a natural buffer between children and their trauma. It increases your child's ability to acknowledge their feelings surrounding the reality and finality of the death at a pace that feels manageable to them. Expressive arts counter the disruption you experience in stress and give your brain a chance to find ways to take care of itself and your body.[1]

As you honor your grief and support your child, remember that when they endure loss involving trauma, they may not have words to describe their experience. Art therapist Cathy Malchiodi describes it like this:

> When we do not have words to convey our sensations, feelings, or thoughts, we cannot simply "name it to tame it." But we can use movement, rhythm, sound, image, and play. The transformative and restorative role of expressive arts provides a voice when language is unavailable or impossible.[2]

Finding a Sense of Safety

When you and your child experience loss with trauma, your physical safety needs to be felt on a sensory level.[3] Before engaging in sensory-based expressive arts, you can cultivate safety and comfort for yourself and your child by assessing your needs before offering a therapeutic activity. You can meet your sensory needs by discovering what you need to feel safe in your space. Attune to your sensory needs by considering lighting levels, the weight of a blanket, the temperature in the room, and your hunger and thirst. Identify any tension in your body and see what you might need in order to increase your felt sense of safety. You can offer your child a snack, a weighted blanket or stuffed animal, or a water bottle to sip.

When you feel threatened by your environment, your body's natural response is to prioritize keeping you safe by suppressing your digestive system. If you were walking in the woods and encountered a bear, you wouldn't sit down to eat a sandwich. Our survival response is a remarkable feature of our brain and its ability to keep us safe. If you are experiencing a stress response but are not in danger, you might try calming your body through chewing, specifically something tangy, sour, minty, chewy, or crunchy. If you are safe enough to eat a snack or chew a piece of gum, you communicate to your brain that you are not in true danger, interrupting the anxiety cycle.

Expression Through the Arts

When you experience trauma, your body's stress response limits your verbal ability because of how it affects the part of your brain (prefrontal cortex) responsible for language. Your body is so good at keeping you safe that when trauma occurs, it prioritizes your survival and activates your freeze, flight, or fight response. Accessing words is more difficult when your survival response is activated. What is stored in your body—grief and trauma—is best expressed through your body. Expressive arts such as the following support healing.

Sand Play

Sand play utilizes miniature objects in a tray of sand to express complex and overwhelming emotions in a nonverbal way. Through miniature objects such as people, fences, animals, and cars, children can create a visual to represent the story inside them. The sand tray acts as a "container" for stories and emotions that feel overwhelming when they are inside of us. Sand play objects serve as metaphors for emotions and relationships. After their time with sand play, children often find insight they didn't have before.

You can re-create the therapeutic activity of sand play with your child by filling up a rectangular cake pan with sand and offering small figures: miniature people, pets, rocks, and everyday objects. Your job is not to analyze or try and make sense of their play but rather to be a noticer. Using a sportscasting approach, which is when you narrate what you see them doing, you can say, "I am noticing you gathered all the dinosaurs in a circle." Your child may respond, "These dinosaurs are safer with their friends." You can then respond to what they've shared with you by reflecting, "Your dinosaurs are safer together."

Dramatic Play

Dramatic play invites children to explore their experiences through actions and objects. In the dramatic playroom at Jessica's House, one child acting as the "genie" offered a magic lamp to another child whose sister died. The "genie" said, "Make a wish." And the other child said, "I wish my sister would come back." The "genie" then donned costume angel wings as he walked over and conveyed nonverbally his desire to fulfill his friend's wish. They honored each other by witnessing one another's pain and expressing what they wished they could change.

You can create opportunities for dramatic play at home with a variety of dress-up clothes and other items that can represent your child's experience. Consider including items like a toy ambulance, fire truck, magic wand, or doctor's kit to deepen their opportunity to transform their trauma through play.

Music

Music allows for deeper access to emotions, so giving your child instruments to play helps them process their feelings in nonverbal ways. Music fosters connections with peers and family and leads to physiological calming effects such as reduced heart rate.[4] One child at Jessica's House whose brother died put words to her loss by creating a song titled, "Where Did You Go?" She gave instruments to her fellow group members and asked them to play along.

Invite your child to create a sound representing a feeling in their body, using a drum or two spoons. Ask open-ended questions such as "What does your anger sound like?" or "What does your worry sound like?" Reflect their rhythm back to them, asking, "Is this how your anger sounds?" Your reflection of their rhythm attunes you through nonverbal conversation.

Community drum circles are also a creative way to express messages and emotions, through both playing drums and moving to the rhythm. Rhythm and drumming help regulate our emotions as we release what is difficult to express. The circle creates a sense of safety and belonging because of a collective experience.

Slow Movement

Engaging in slow body movements like swinging, swaying, or yoga calms your nervous system and brings you back into your body and to the present moment. Swinging helps increase blood flow to the brain, supporting focus and calming anxiety.[5] You can increase your mind-body connection through yoga practice. Yoga promotes feelings of emotional, physical, and psychological safety by increasing body awareness. And doing yoga poses like Warrior Two can elicit inner strength.

Ask your child to take a form in their body that takes up as much space as possible and feels sturdy, solid, or ready for action. One activity for power posing is to ask your child to create a pose that represents a feeling in their body and then transform themselves into the opposite. "Show me what worry looks like in your body. Now show me what strength looks like."

Big Muscle Movements

Going outdoors provides a space for engaging your child's body with big muscle movements. Activities that require focus and attention give their brain a break from worries they might have about what happened or what might happen next. Activities like bouncing a basketball, kicking a soccer ball, catching or throwing, bopping a balloon in the air back and forth, or playing Ping-Pong help stimulate brain connectivity. It's hard to worry while concentrating on catching or hitting a ball or balloon. Climbing on play structures or walking along a curb challenges balance and engages your child in safe, risk-taking play. Engaging in safe risks facilitates a healthy level of discomfort as they work through a challenge and complete the task at hand. Successfully working through such challenges and tasks fosters resiliency, building your child's capacity for healing.

Grounding and Mindfulness

When you are activated and are experiencing a stress response, you aren't fully present and connected with your body. Grounding yourself is one way to reconnect with your body, reducing fear or panic. You can ground yourself by becoming aware of your body and the environment around you. Look at your hands and lightly touch the back of your left hand with your right fingers, then do the same on the other side. If you are sitting, rub your thighs with the palms of your hands. Look around and notice your environment. Name five things you see (the color of the wall, the number of windows in the room), four things you hear (birds outside, people talking), three things you feel (the weight of your body in your chair, your feet on the ground), two things you smell (this book in your hands), and one thing you taste. Try mindfulness and grounding with your child by going on a walk outdoors, perhaps taking a sensory walk in a garden—feeling the sun on your skin, touching the dirt with your fingers, smelling the flowers, and hearing birds chirping. Observe for yourself and ask your child, "What do you smell, taste, touch, see, hear?"

Supporting Your Child

Your child may need to explore their empowerment and learn ways to respond to threats in an aggressive and healthy way. Healthy aggression leads us to a sense of mastery and feeling more competent.[6] Open your hands and stretch your arms away from your body. Breathe in, and as you do, bring your hands toward your heart as you inhale what brings you strength. Your hands are also there to push away what isn't helpful. Thrust your hands and arms out slowly and forcefully, as if meeting resistance. Exhale what isn't helping you and what you want to move away from you. You can use your hands in a healthy aggressive way to shield yourself and sweep away harm.

Your child may want to use their hands and feet to act out their anger at cancer—or their voice to yell at it. They may want to stomp their feet when they fear a monster in their closet or any other threat that reminds them of their loss. They can use their hands to push away worry that something else bad might happen. By using their feet to kick and voice to yell, they are finding ways to skillfully counter a threat. When their body moves in a way that helps them feel empowered, it helps to move them out of an immobile (freeze) response.

As your child explores different expressions and coping skills, they will notice what feels right for them. The more they discover empowerment, the more accessible these resources become in their time of need.

Your Own Expression

What experiences do you hold that are longing to be expressed? You may have absorbed messages from childhood or over time that said you aren't an artist. Perhaps you were told you were too loud or that it's not okay to cry. These messages can suppress your creative ways of communicating what needs to be released. Acknowledge your inner critic and quiet its voice before engaging with the expressive arts. Expression is not about perfection. It's about feeling what you need to feel in this moment and expressing it in some way so you can heal.

Hand over heart, dear reader. Deep breath in.
Let it out. Say aloud, "I give myself compassion
as I learn what I need to do to express myself."

HEALING PRACTICES

Reflection

1. Think back to when you were a child. Which of the expressive arts activities mentioned above would you have enjoyed? Which ones would you consider incorporating into your life today?

2. Draw a tree with a root system. Notice what's underground holding you up. Your root system could be your connectedness to God, your friends and family, and strengths you have developed through other tragedies in your life. List what gives you strength and keeps you connected.

3. What else do you want to add to your root system to give yourself additional support?

Expressive Arts Invitation: Volcano Room

Design an "erupting volcano" space in your home by creating a place for expressing explosive emotions. Depending on your child's age and abilities, try:

Throwing clay

Stomping on bubble wrap

Hitting pillows

Blowing up and popping paper bags

Tearing paper

Hitting a mat with a foam pool noodle

Lifting something heavy

Pushing on an immovable object like a wall

Throwing ice cubes against a hard outdoor surface

Expressive Arts Invitation: Shield of Strength

Supplies needed: paper or cardboard, aluminum foil, and markers or crayons

Cut out a shield of paper or cardboard and cover both sides with foil. On one side, invite your child to write or draw what they want to deflect. This can include fears or messages from others they don't want to absorb. On the other side, invite them to write or draw their strengths. Include who or what brings them strength, like encouraging words they want to hold close to their heart. Have them hold the shield with the strength side toward their body so what they want to deflect is facing away from them.

Discussion Questions with Your Child

1. What do you want to shield yourself from and push away?
2. What strengths and comforting messages do you want to bring close to your heart?

A Blessing for Expression

Splatter the colors of your heart on the wall
Show the hollowness of your life without them
The chasm between what was and what is
The parts of you that died with them

And the parts that are new
Move in a way that shows what it feels like to be missing them
Play their laugh with chopsticks on your plate
Take your story
Stir it into paint
And brush it across the sky

11

Facing Holidays and Other Milestones

Carter died at the end of September, and we were quickly greeted by spooky season. Yards turned into cemeteries. Blood and gore. Skeletons. What previously never bothered me increased my darkness. Warm days turned into cold, long nights, and this year the cozy season, always my favorite, tightened around me with a shroud of dread.

As the holidays approached, I heard of friends and family taking their Christmas photos. Soon their cards would arrive in the mail. The thought of intact families with messages of cheer crushed me. One day I told my friend, "I want to burn my Christmas cards." Later that week, her card arrived in the mail. On the outside of the envelope, she wrote, "BURN MINE FIRST" in bold black letters. She held space for my resentment. I wanted my family back.

On our fourth fall without Carter, I noticed more beauty in the changing season. More wonder. I found the energy to host Thanksgiving dinner for the first time since his death. I woke early and wrestled the turkey into the roasting pan. The wafting scents of sage and thyme mingled with the sound of the parade blaring in the background to spark possibility.

Glimmers of warmth and gratitude infused with longing draped the empty places. I scurried to find a sense of home for the holidays. A curated Thanksgiving playlist? Check. Everyone's favorite foods? Yep. Candles lit? Done. Our arriving guests would be looking for home as much as I was.

I noticed the weight of missing Carter on the shoulders of each person who walked through the door. A flicker of his vacancy in their eyes. His absence was still the loudest voice in the room. But we tried. We circled. Held hands around the kitchen island. Gave thanks. Sat at the candlelit table and excavated current events as children sparked levity among the hollowness.

We are finding our crooked way home.

The holidays can intensify the grief you carry. You may feel a sense of dread and miss the holiday warmth, wonder, and joy you had before your loved one died. Perhaps the holidays have always held pressure and stress for you, and your loss makes facing this season feel impossible. Someone else carving the turkey, an empty stocking, or your person missing as you light your Hanukkah candles are painful reminders of their absence and all that has changed.

Although your loved one is physically absent from celebrations, you can continue to honor their memory. Welcome ideas from your child. After her husband died, one mom said, "We held a quiet gathering with our close family the first year after his death. Instead of our extended family gathering, we connected through a video call." One dad whose wife died said, "We have a moment of silence each year to remember my wife during our holiday meal." Another said, "Every New Year's Eve, we go around the room sharing what we miss about my wife and end by making a toast in her honor."

You can decide if you wish to extend invitations to family and friends to join these opportunities to remember your loved one. After the holidays, check in with your family. Ask your child what worked for them and what didn't. Explore ideas of what can be done differently during the next holiday season.

When the person you love is no longer physically with you, holiday activities like decorating and gift buying may feel unbearable. One mom said she had to let go of "making the magic happen" during the holidays. She minimized the decorations and scaled down her traditional family festivities. As invitations arrive for holiday events, ask yourself if the gathering will be energizing or draining for you. Communicate if the responsibilities you once held feel like too much now. When you receive a holiday invitation, take a moment to reflect on how you are feeling. What do you notice in your body when you imagine attending? You can look to your body as a communicator. Do you feel a green light to accept the invitation? Or a sinking feeling telling you no? You may have initial reservations or affirmations about accepting an invitation, so consider waiting before responding. Perhaps you'll feel differently when you give yourself time for consideration. Or it will solidify your decision that it's better to decline or accept.

You can decline with a simple response, such as, "Thank you for the invite. We would appreciate one in the future, but we're not up for it this year." If you wish to accept an invitation, having a flexible plan can assure you of an exit strategy if needed. You may want to leave a holiday gathering early or not go at all, even if you previously accepted the invitation. Saying "I plan to attend but can only stay a short time," helps you anticipate your needs. If you go, give yourself permission to take a break or leave when necessary. Taking a walk, stepping into another room, or going outside for fresh air can help you to your next moment. Perhaps you can drive separately from other guests if you want to leave early. If possible, bring a friend who can provide extra support. Ask your friend to communicate with the host if you need to leave early.

Only you know what is best during this time. Release yourself from the pressure to make others happy. You can try something different one year and return to previous traditions the next. Instead of attending a large family gathering, you may wish to stay home or go somewhere else. Rather than preparing the traditional holiday dinner, you may want to pick up takeout. After her husband died, one mom explained, "My husband loved hosting, but I don't. After he died, I felt the pressure to keep everything the same. I finally was honest with my family that hosting isn't something I enjoy. I was surprised at how understanding everyone was. It was a relief to be myself and not the person I thought I should be." As you make decisions about the holidays, trust your inner wisdom to choose what is best for you and your child.

Grief impacts your body and mind, and rest is essential for your healing, especially during the holidays. Create opportunities to rest during this frenzied season. You might plan quiet evenings at home with a family movie night or end your day with a walk or gentle stretching.

The cheerful nature and expectations of holidays clash with the sorrow you are holding. Where there used to be the buzz of holiday spirit, your energy is now channeled to adjusting to these important days without your loved one's presence. They were the object of your generosity during the holidays. Now they are no longer here, and your energy of love has nowhere to go. Because your person can no longer physically receive and reciprocate your devotion, it returns to you as emptiness and sorrow. One mom remarked, "I always loved seeing my son's face when he opened his gifts on Christmas. I enjoyed the process of talking with him about his Christmas list and shopping for the gift he would love the most. Christmas morning feels so empty without him, and it's hard to watch our daughter open her gifts without her brother by her side."

As you move through winter holidays and face the New Year, you may have conflicted feelings. One mom said, "When the New Year approached, I felt like I was leaving my daughter behind because she died that year. It was so hard to move into a new year without her." A dad whose wife died voiced, "This year was the worst experience of my life. I felt so relieved that it was over." One family watched the sunset together on the last day of the year, wishing for better days ahead.

Be especially gentle with yourself this season. Holidays are often filled with expectation and disappointment even without grief, and grieving during the holidays can render them grueling.

Birthdays

How did your loved one like to celebrate their birthday? How do you want to remember them now? One mom started a memorial garden in a small area of her yard and still adds to it each year on her son's birthday and death anniversary. She explained, "Every year I gather with close family and friends, and we weed his garden and plant new plants in memory of him." One dad honors his wife's birthday by taking a family hike each year, saying, "We drive to her favorite trail, pack her favorite foods, and share memories about her during lunch." Some families like to remember their person's forever age and keep that many candles on their loved one's cake, and others celebrate what age they would be in the current year. After her daughter died, one mom began donating a toy she thought her daughter would have liked on her birthday each year.

Death Anniversaries

The anniversary of your loved one's death is another day to consider honoring. You may notice that as the day approaches, you begin to feel anxious or have a deepening sense of loss. You may find your body remembering, with the weather and time of year contributing to similar feelings from the season in which they died. One dad called September his "scorched" month after his son's death, while another called the anniversary of the death their "heaven day." One mom whose daughter died said, "I give myself permission to feel lousy. I take time off work a few days before and after the 'crapiversary' of my daughter's death." Some families like to gather at

113

their loved one's grave or ash scattering site. While there, some hold lit candles while taking turns sharing something they miss or will never forget. Others bring their loved one's favorite snack or drink to share during the visit. One mom said, "I write a letter each year to my husband, telling him of all the happenings from the previous year. I plan to share them with my children as they grow."

Returning to the place where you experienced the burial of your loved one can stir up memories and feelings within you. One dad remarked, "Why would I want to think about and relive the worst day of my life? I don't feel a connection with her there. She's everywhere." Give thought to whether visiting the gravesite will bring you and your child comfort. Only you can decide what is true for you.

It's understandable if you don't wish to recognize and remember their death anniversary. One mom said, "My husband's death anniversary is too painful. I like to honor him on his birthday and Father's Day." As you consider what feels best for your family, ask yourself if honoring the death anniversary will feel helpful or hurtful. And remember, what you decide to do one year can change the next. Honor yourself. You never expected to make decisions like these.

Other Milestones

Other days that may feel especially heavy are milestones that happen without them, such as graduations and weddings. Holidays such as New Year's Eve, Easter, Passover, Mother's Day and Father's Day, and summer holidays like the Fourth of July can also be tough. You may feel the emotion building as the day gets closer and then peaking and receding as you move through these important days. One mom said, "The anticipation of the day was harder than the day itself. Somehow, I got through the days I thought would be the most difficult."

You may be surprised by the effect of other calendar events such as filing taxes and having to list yourself as a widow or decrease your number of dependents. If your loved one was an avid football fan, the traditions you shared on Super Bowl Sunday won't feel the same. Other times that may strike you unexpectedly hard include three-day holiday weekends and the end of daylight saving time, extending the darkness of the night.

Supporting Your Child

As you talk with your child about the approaching holidays or other milestones, invite their thoughts and questions by asking, "With the holidays coming, how would you like to celebrate?" They may wonder if the holidays will hold to the same customs or if you will build new traditions. One mom said they decided as a family that her son's stocking would become a memory stocking. "Each person in the family wrote a memory throughout the holiday season and put it in the stocking, and we read them together on Christmas Eve." The holidays were still agonizing, but she was glad they found a way to include him.

You may find that your child misses their loved one while also being excited about their favorite parts of the holidays. Remind your child that it is healthy to hold different emotions at the same time.

Invite your family's ideas on what each person values for their holidays. One child may want to keep as many traditions as possible, while another may wish to try something new. One might want to spend time with extended family, while another may find it stressful to be with a large group. A traditional holiday dinner with your loved one's favorite foods may be a priority for one, while another may want to volunteer at a community kitchen. Explore together how to respect each other's values while meeting individual needs, even when it feels like nothing is quite right or good. Finding compromises can help each person feel honored during this season. If a compromise isn't possible, you can pause and revisit ideas in the following years. As one mom noted, "The first year after my husband died, it felt too hard to join our extended family's holiday traditions. I decided to opt out altogether. Maybe another year I'll want to join."

115

Honoring Your Love

As you mourn the holidays and other milestones without your loved one, honor your love for them. It can take time to find ways to re-member them, and what fits today will likely change next year. Trust you will not always feel the way you do right now.

Hand over heart, dear reader. Deep breath in. Let it out. Say aloud, "I give myself the compassion I need as I face important days without them."

HEALING PRACTICES

Reflection

1. Which holiday or milestone is the most challenging for you?
2. As you think about your plans for an upcoming holiday, what is important to you?

Expressive Arts Invitation: Remembering Your Loved One During the Holidays

- Light a memorial candle.
- Select an ornament.
- Place their favorite flower on the table.
- Make a toast in their memory.
- Visit the grave or ash scattering site.
- Make their favorite food.
- Share memories around the table.
- Display photos of them.

Discussion Questions with Your Child

1. What holiday traditions do you want to keep this year?
2. What holiday traditions do you want to skip this year?

Family Candlelight Ceremony

Come together to light four candles in memory of your loved one, and read this script:

*We light this candle for the **emptiness** we feel without you. The pain of missing you reminds us of the depth of our love for you. We wish you were here with us, and we remember you.*

We light this candle in your **memory**. We will never forget the times we laughed or disagreed, the fun times, or the memories we made. We carry you with us, always.

We light this candle for **hope**. We remind ourselves that feelings are not forever. When living without you feels like too much, may we trust we will feel hopeful again.

We light this candle for **love**. We remember our love for you and yours for us. May the love you brought to this world shine in us for each other.

As we acknowledge the **emptiness** and honor your **memory**, may we find moments of **hope** and gratitude for the light of your **love**.

A Blessing for Your Holidays without Them

When you come to the day
The one you didn't want to face
Without them
When the stocking is empty
And so is their chair

When their absence presses in
And you wonder how to breathe
May you sense a filling
In the sunken places

As you miss them in the room and in your soul
May solace find you

As you survive your day
May the sharing of your sorrow give you rest
When you say, "She would have loved this"
May others nod in witness

May you find the strength to live in the hollow
And trust you will do it again

12

Returning to Work and School

I took family leave after Carter died and stepped away from my role as director of Jessica's House. Work has always felt like a sacred calling for me, but nothing else seemed to matter after Carter's death. It felt weird to be the director of a grief center and have my son die. Maybe I secretly thought if I kept busy helping other people, a loss like this wouldn't touch me.

A few months after Carter's death, I sat with my beloved counselor and she said, "You really light up when you talk about your work," and I thought, Maybe I'm ready. I knew I didn't have the capacity to support others in their grief, but we were in the middle of a building project and pouring energy into a meaningful and creative venture felt manageable.

In January 2020, I eased back into work—only to go home in March when COVID-19 shifted the world. Grieving during the pandemic felt especially disorienting. I held the tension of the pain of the world with widespread uncertainty and grief. At the same time, I found comfort in hunkering down with our family for a while during such a tender time. Slower days helped us preserve our limited energy.

My daughter Camille came home from college during that time, and being together brought us strength. We had just dropped her off for her freshman year at college the day before Carter's accident. Calling her about the accident when she didn't have support around her crushed us. She flew home and arrived at the hospital just in time to say goodbye to her brother. She stayed home for the rest of that quarter as we healed together.

Camille returned to school in 2021. She found supportive roommates and settled into her new rhythm at school. I went back to work in person to prepare for our grand opening.

There are still workdays that feel like too much. Times when I cry. And lunches when I drive away and nap in my car so I can face the rest of my day. I am learning to hold the sacredness of my lifework alongside my grief.

W hen your person dies, nothing else matters, yet everyday responsibilities continue. You may wonder, *How can the world keep spinning when mine has stopped?* As impossible as it may feel, there will come a time when you return to work and your child to school. Even during your most difficult days, household chores, home and car repairs, meal prep, homework help, and work are still there, demanding your attention.

Returning to Work

You may be overwhelmed by the idea of going back to work. Or you may have already returned, perhaps far before you felt ready. You may find work stabilizing, as it gives you a familiar routine. One dad said, "My work gave me a reason to get up most mornings. It kept me moving and motivated to keep stepping forward." Another mentioned, "It felt hard to face my coworkers the first day, but they were supportive, and I felt reassured when they told me more about their lives and losses than I knew before."

As you prepare to return to work, consider writing an email to help others know what to expect and what you need. You can tell them what helps and what doesn't. One mom asked for what she needed (and what she didn't need): "I asked my employer to inform my coworkers that I didn't want any sentiments with platitudes like 'God never gives you more than you can handle.' I received many thoughtful messages from my coworkers that didn't contain clichés. Because they avoided words aimed at making me (and themselves) feel better, their sentiments felt more authentic." Another mom said, "The weekend before I returned to work, my coworkers and I met. It made going back a little easier because we already had our first conversations out of the way."

You are not returning to work as the same person you were before your loved one died, and you likely don't have the capacity to function in the ways you did before the death. If possible, consider taking a leave of absence from work. Check in with your company's HR department and ask about their policies on bereavement leave and benefits, if necessary.

If your spouse died, you are now holding the responsibilities at home as a solo parent in addition to trying to meet the demands of work. If the idea of making it through an entire workday seems unmanageable, try asking your employer if you could ease into work with modified hours for a time. If a schedule change is not possible, plan breaks throughout your day to make room for what seems doable. One dad said, "I learned to schedule extra time between meetings because I was so exhausted and needed to take a break."

Grief goes with you into your workday. The complaints you hear from coworkers may now sound trivial. Your outlook on the world has changed. You may have little patience for small talk and workplace grumblings as you are clawing your way through your days carrying your loss.

Grief impacts your cognitive function, including your memory and concentration, so don't hold yourself to the performance standards you once did. One mom said, "I noticed my emails and documents contained small mistakes that were not normal for me. I asked my coworker to look over my work, and she was glad to support me in that way." It's natural for your brain to have altered patterns as you learn to live without your person. Intrusive and wandering thoughts are common when your grief needs your attention. Instead of pushing away your thoughts, try writing them down. You are doing the hard work of mourning when you are both on and off the job.

Know you will have times when work feels impossible and other times when work may feel like the relief you need. One mom said, "After my husband died, I was surprised at how easy it was at first to throw myself into work. Looking back, I think I was numb, and it was the distraction I was looking for. But as time went on, I realized there was no way to keep the pace I once did." Another noted, "After my son died, I found my priorities changing. Work didn't feel as important as before. I found myself wanting to quit."

Your grief will at times be loud and at other times be quiet. You may sense a lack of motivation or find yourself more irritable than usual. You could have difficulty making decisions that once felt easy. You might forget meetings or miss deadlines. When your grief is loud, find a safe place to cry. Crying releases endorphins and oxytocin, which are natural pain relievers and mood boosters. Tears release tension, regulating your nervous system and shifting you into a more relaxed and calmer state.[1]

Napping can also help reduce the stress and tension that naturally build up during your workday, especially if you aren't sleeping well.[2] Be gentle with yourself during your transition. Your normal sleep patterns can take years to return after losing a spouse or child. Because grief elevates the stress hormone cortisol, it's common for high levels of cortisol to disrupt your sleep.[3] Sleeplessness impacts how you feel physically and emotionally. One mom said, "I keep a pillow in my car along with my favorite snacks and water. I know it's a place to go during my workday when I need to recharge."

Think about ways you can surround yourself with self-care and comfort. Perhaps you want to bring in plants for life and oxygen to your workspace or have your favorite mug at your desk. Switching some of your meetings to walking meetings can help expel some of the energy of grief you carry. Incorporate stretching and breathing and consider listening to calming music as you work. Use your lunch breaks to care for yourself in the middle of your day. One mom voiced, "When I'm having a hard time, I will either call a friend or take a walk during my lunch break." Playing a quick game on your phone like Tetris or doodling a repetitive pattern like a Zentangle can give your brain a break, helping you to stay more present during trauma-related intrusive thoughts.[4] Give yourself something to look forward to after work, such as a walk or dinner with a friend.

Supporting Your Child

Before your child returns to school, inform their teacher of the death so they can provide extra support. Discuss extensions on completing schoolwork to ease any unnecessary pressure. Plan to inform new teachers about the loss your family has experienced at the beginning of every school year. One teacher said, "It's helpful for me to know if a child has experienced a death in their family, even if it happened years ago. I want to be sensitive to their loss and keep it in mind as I plan activities throughout the year." Let their teacher know what days may be difficult and if you and your child plan to take time off during significant dates such as the death anniversary or birthdays.

Ask your child's teacher to talk to the class about how to support their grieving friend. Explain that when a person is grieving, they don't want to be treated differently and still like to have fun. Ask the students to include their friend who is grieving in activities they enjoyed together before the death. Let the class know it can be helpful if they say, "I'm here for you." Explain that their friend might like to share memories and talk about the person who died. Knowing what not to say is also helpful. After her mom died, one child said, "I don't like it when my friends say, 'I know just how you feel.' They have no idea how I feel. They still have their mom."

Children grieving a death often find it difficult to concentrate in school or engage in the everyday activities they did before the person died. Children often don't want to be different, so they may not talk about the death. Another reason they may not talk about the death is out of fear of crying in front of their peers. They may naturally withdraw from their friendships or activities for a time.

Some children can feel left out or alone at school when they're grieving. If your child reports that their classmates are acting unkind toward them, listen to and validate your child. Help them practice responses like using their words to say "Stop," walking away, finding others to be with, or talking with an adult at school. Discuss strategies with their teacher so they can take firm action and perhaps enlist another peer to help your child feel supported.

The death of your loved one can change your child's sense of security, and being separated from you may be distressing. They may be preoccupied with thoughts about your safety and well-being during their school day. One mom mentioned her child experienced separation anxiety after the death of her sister and struggled to be away from her parents. "I started drawing a heart on my daughter's hand before school, and she drew a heart on mine. I told her when she looked at her heart to remember I am with her, and she is with me."

When you say goodbye before school, and other times when you will be apart for a while, tell your child where you are going, what you will be doing, and when you will be back. Plan with the school staff so your child knows they can call you during their lunch or recess break to check in if needed.

Perhaps your child's teacher can work with them to develop a system that makes it easier to communicate when they need extra support. Some teachers find it helpful to give a student a small deck of sticky notes to place on their desk to signal when they need extra support. Ask if there is a counselor or peer group to help your child at school. Perhaps there is a place like a comfort corner where your child can take a break with calming music, books, or a weighted blanket. If your child's energy of grief feels big, perhaps they can go outdoors to run. Moving the energy of anxiety out of their bodies helps them return to their "just-right" place so they can focus on learning.

As you and your child find your rhythm of work and school, know there is no right or wrong way to hold your grief alongside your responsibilities.

Hand over heart, dear reader. Deep breath in. Let it out. Say aloud, "May I give myself the compassion I need as I learn to hold my grief and my responsibilities."

HEALING PRACTICES

Reflection

1. What do you wish your coworkers knew about your grief?
2. What helps you through your workday?

For Your Child

Since my person died, school has been _____.
I wish my teachers would understand that _____
_____.
I wish my friends knew that _____.

Expressive Arts Invitation: My Animal's Safe Place

Supplies needed: small box and modeling dough

Ask your child to create an animal with modeling dough. After they create their animal, ask, "What does your animal need to feel safe?" Create items from the dough that help their animal feel safe, such as food, grass, water, friends/family, or toys. Place the items inside the box with their animal.

Power Posing

Together with your child, according to your and your child's age and ability, try power posing to reduce feelings of anxiety and worry about returning to school and work. Power posing impacts our feelings of confidence.[5] As you and your child prepare to return to work and school, practice power poses together. Try these for two minutes before you leave for the day, or before facing a stressful event.

Pose 1: Strike a pose like a superhero. Spread your legs two feet apart and puff out your chest. Put your hands into fists and place them on your hips like Wonder Woman.

Pose 2: Pretend you just scored a game-winning goal or won a race. Push your chest out and raise your arms like a "V" into the air in victory.

Pose 3: While sitting, link your fingers and place them behind your head, so your elbows are facing out away from each side of your body. Lean back and stretch your legs out. Take up as much space as possible.

Discussion Questions with Your Child

1. What helps you feel better during your school day?
2. Who can you talk to about your worries?

A Blessing for Work

May your heart guide you
To know when or if it is time
To return to your work

To bless the life you are building
To engage your pursuit, your craft
What makes you feel alive needs you

Your gifts, your time, the sacredness and beauty of you
Because only you can bring you

May you find a closet to cry in
May coworkers become your truest friends

May creativity and your sacred calling
Be your restoration

May you be fulfilled
And may your dreams and possibilities renew you

13

Being with Your Difficult Emotions

I was scrolling through social media when I saw a photo of one of Carter's friends who got engaged. I gasped out loud. I wasn't expecting such a strong reaction, but there it was. I cried hot, jealous tears as envy exploded in me.

It's hard for me to admit, but I'm jealous.

Shortly after Carter died, I began meeting with friends who had also lost a child. We called ourselves the Dead Kids Club and told tales we would never share with others outside this club we never wanted to join. One late summer, we noticed parents who were sad because their kids were going to college. We wanted to yell, "BUT YOU WILL SEE THEM AGAIN!"

It's not like I want any of my friends' kids to never go to college or get married, but it's a harsh reminder of the shattering of my hopes and dreams for Carter. For our family. These passages of adulthood we were preparing him for.

I want him here. I want HIM.

Jealousy reflects my protest.

He was mine.
And I want him back.
It's not enough to hold on to my memories or have him show up as
a butterfly.
I want him skin and bones.
Like other peoples' sons.

Some emotions in grief are difficult to admit when you're griev-ing in a culture that values positivity. Yet these emotions are part of the transformative pain of your grief. Jealousy and rage attempt to assert power and control, and regret or shame rep-resent your vulnerability. Often these emotions conflict, like never wishing suffering upon someone else while having a strong desire to be understood and for others to feel your pain the way you do.

Jealousy and Envy

The ache for what you've lost may show up as jealousy or envy, which may feel like bad emotions yet are common in grief. You wish you had what someone else still has. Jealousy is a common reaction to loss and connects you to your desire for your life to be different than it is right now. It's not a "dirty" emotion, yet it can be cultur-ally unacceptable to express. As you acknowledge jealousy, know it's understandable to protest what you wish you still had. Some people call envy the "unrecognized part of grief." It's an honest plea to have the part of you that is missing your person be witnessed.

Just like with other emotions, jealousy comes with contradictory feelings. You can value your relationship and still be jealous of what you no longer have. Your feelings of jealousy are a testament to your love and pain. One mom said she feels jealous when hearing about someone who survived something that her child didn't. She added, "When I hear of someone who was rescued and recovered from drowning, my first reaction is anger. Like, why was her child rescued and not mine? And at the same time, I would never want anyone to experience my anguish."

One teen shared that he not only feels jealous when he sees another kid with their mom but also feels angry if they are not being kind to her. "I hate it when I see someone taking their mom for granted when I would do anything to have mine back." One young adult whose dad died voiced, "It's hard for me when I hear my friend's dad giving him advice when I have so many questions for my own. I need my dad right now with the choices I'm making with my career and interviews. He would know what to do."

Everyday moments can activate feelings of envy. Seeing someone who still has their partner or child reminds you of what you'll miss forever. If you see a couple together, or a friend tells you about their child's milestone birthday party or graduation, it may take your breath away. One mom commented that after her child died, it was torture to attend birthday parties for her child's cousins. She added, "I didn't want to be left out. Going was brutal, but not being invited was just as severe." Another mom and dad remarked that after their daughter died, they began searching for some new friends: "It was just easier not to always be with our friends whose children are the same age as our daughter would be."

Feelings of jealousy and envy are rooted in expressing how life is unfair. Jealousy is an unspoken question begging for an answer to why there is such inequality in the world. It screams, "I didn't deserve this injustice." Just like your other reactions to loss, jealousy must be acknowledged and expressed. When one person's child dies and another's lives, it's not fair. When one person's spouse lives long, and they celebrate their fiftieth anniversary when you only celebrated five years, it's not fair. Express feelings of jealousy without judgment—you are learning to live with the reminders of your loss as you see others have what once was yours. The space between is painful as you see your peers in the place you once were and always hoped to be.

Relief

Relief is the ease of suffering when what is painful stops. If your loved one suffered through an illness, you may find relief that they are no longer in pain. You may be met with feelings of shame or guilt for feeling relieved.

If the death was by accidental overdose or fentanyl poisoning, your loved one may have been living with the illness of addiction. One dad said fearing the news of an overdose suspended him in a state of dread. His hope was that his son would recover, but instead the son died. After his son's death, he experienced relief mingled with sadness. He said, "We prayed for years for our son's recovery, and there were times I thought we were close. Now I know he will no longer find wholeness here on the earth, and I'm devastated. And I'm also relieved he has finally found peace and rest."

Some relationships are unhealthy or even abusive, and the grief that follows the death is confusing because it may be the first time you've felt safe in a long while. You may wish you had a chance to see the person change and heal, but instead they died. As you hold your desire for a different outcome alongside your relief that they can't hurt you anymore, remember that your feelings of relief don't minimize the enormity of your loss.

Guilt, Shame, and Blame

Part of your brain's way of keeping you safe is to find out how someone died. Our brains acclimate to threats in our environment, and we teach our children safety based on our understanding of what happened to others in the past. Our desire for this information is an attempt to keep ourselves and others safe in a similar circumstance. If we know how it happened, maybe we can prevent it from happening to us.

When your loss involves trauma, your brain responds automatically to keep you alive by activating your freeze, flight, or fight mechanisms. Remember that your response is rooted in strength, not weakness. You would not be alive if it wasn't for your body's survival response. Yet so much of the time we shame ourselves for our reactions, even though they are automatic. In that natural, unrelenting search for why and how, it's also natural to blame yourself or others for the death. Know that most times those thoughts soften as they are felt and expressed.

You may find yourself living in the realm of "What if?" or "If only." "What if he left five minutes later?" "If only I insisted she go see the doctor." Your internal questions are another way your brain is attempting to make sense of what happened as you ponder every possibility. Just as you can't talk yourself out of a feeling before it is felt, you can't talk yourself out of these what-ifs until you have allowed yourself to sit with them. Trust in your natural process and that, in time, you will learn to live instead in the "What *is*."

If your child died, your relationship with your partner can be deeply affected. Shame and blame may be at the top of your emotions. Since you are charged with your child's safety from birth, anything that happens to them can feel like it's your fault, even when you know it's not. Notice and acknowledge the presence of shame and blame. If it's helpful, create a script for yourself when these thoughts overwhelm reason. A father whose child died in an accident while in his care created the script "It was an accident." He repeated this to himself during surges of shame and blame.

Guilt is often an emotion that others don't want you to feel. If you express your guilt, you may be met with, "It's not your fault." Yet guilt is another common feeling in grief that needs to be validated and integrated. As with other parts of your grief, you will notice your guilt building, peaking, and receding.

Guilt is rooted in our desire to have order in our life. We search for answers and reasons why our person died because it's easier than accepting that the world is unpredictable. There must be someone to blame for our person dying. Even if it's ourselves. Our desire to control the outcome can point the blame back to us.

One dad whose son died said, "There are so many things I wish I would have done differently as a dad, and sometimes I think if I would have done those things, my son would be alive. But I'm working through my regrets. I like to say that I drive through my guilt and park for a little while, but I don't stay there forever."

When Grief Gets Competitive or Dismissed

Who else is grieving the loss of your loved one? Your children, parents, in-laws, friends, and other extended family members are also grieving. Because it's natural to want to feel understood, each person affected desires others to know how much they're hurting. For some, the wish for others to understand their pain means they feel and express that *their* loss is the most difficult. They may believe their loss is more devastating somehow because of their unique relationship with your loved one. The competition of who is hurting the most dismisses and invalidates your shared pain.

Or perhaps you've stepped aside and given your need to grieve to someone else. After their miscarriage, one dad shared that he believed his wife deserved more support, as she was the one who'd carried their child. He added, "I placed my feelings on hold and neglected my own loss."

As each person finds their own ways of healing, bring awareness to times when grief becomes competitive or dismissed. Each of you had a distinct relationship with your loved one, and everyone's grief will be uniquely theirs. Find ways to honor each person's grief as you are all mourning your loss in a distinct way.

Supporting Your Child

Support your child as they explore their difficult emotions by normalizing common feelings of grief. Affirm universal grief reactions like anger, jealousy, relief, and guilt by assuring your child that those feelings are widely held not only by you but also by others who are grieving. Gently hold their emotions with them as they process the ones they may feel are "bad." Welcome their honest expressions and reflect their sentiments. If they express jealousy, you can say, "It's not fair they have their dad and you don't have yours. You want your dad back. I want him back too." Or "It's hard to see your friend playing with his sister. You wish your sister were still here. I wish she were here too." Your acceptance and normalization of your child's emotions show it's understandable to feel whatever they feel.

Your child may also hold a sense of responsibility for the death. A child's inner world is a place where magical thinking can cause them to feel like somehow they have the power to cause or prevent death. Their search for how things could have turned out differently is their wish for safety.

Explain to your child that feelings of guilt don't mean they are guilty but rather are the brain's way of making sense of the death. It *feels* safer to think they or someone else caused the death than to live in the randomness of an unpredictable world. They also may experience guilt if they feel relief. After his sister died following a long illness, one child expressed relief that he wouldn't be spending more time in the hospital. He added, "I spent my birthday in the hospital with my sister. Now I feel guilty because I didn't want to be there, and now she's gone."

As your child explores difficult emotions, they may express ones that are hard for you, as their parent, to hear. Yet rescuing them doesn't allow for the necessary processing they need to move through their range of emotions. If your child expresses their guilt and even feels like the death is their fault, instead of quickly responding, "It's not your fault," try, "You feel like the death is your fault. Those are hard words to say." When you accept their full experience of expressing difficult emotions, you become a trusted person who welcomes whatever grief reactions need their attention.

You can't talk someone out of difficult emotions. If you attempt to rescue them by saying, "It's not your fault," you may stop the conversation, leaving them alone in their processing. As you invite their difficult emotions, you can help them access their inner logic by asking questions like, "What would you say to someone else with a loss like yours?" You can also remind them of accurate information about how bodies stop working by saying, "Words and thoughts can't cause another person's body to stop working."

Let Your Emotions Guide You

As you learn to be with your most difficult emotions and support your child with theirs, trust the natural process of brewing, peaking, and receding to guide you in what needs to be felt and expressed. As you stay in the flow of sensing and expressing, you are integrating your loss and finding your healing path.

Hand over heart, dear reader. Deep breath in.
Let it out. Say aloud, "I bring compassion to myself
as I learn to be with my difficult emotions."

HEALING PRACTICES

Reflection

1. What difficult emotions have you felt?
2. What helps you bring awareness to the full spectrum of your emotions?
3. What do you need to express your difficult emotions?

Write a letter to the person who died with these prompts:

- I'm sorry that _____ .
- I wish I could change _____ .
- I wish you _____ .
- I wish I _____ .
- I regret _____ .
- I am learning to forgive you for _____ .
- I am learning to forgive myself for _____ .

Expressive Arts Invitation: Naming and Taming Difficult Emotions

Supplies needed: paper and paint, oil pastels, or skinny markers

Together with your child, talk about a time when you experienced emotions that are hard to admit in grief like jealousy, envy, relief, and regret. Using paint, oil pastels, or skinny markers, draw images of your difficult emotions. You can simply make marks and designs on your paper using shapes and lines to depict your emotions. Scan your body from head to toe. Where in your body do you feel your emotions? If your emotions could talk, what would they say? Write your emotions, questions, or statements on your paper too. Give your emotions a name.

Push your emotions out of your body by placing your fists by your heart, then punching them out to the sides with a big "Ha!" sound. Keep doing it until it feels like you're done. Then press your open hands over your heart and say this mantra: "My difficult emotions represent my love and loss."

Discussion Questions with Your Child

1. What emotion is the hardest for you to feel?
2. What helps you move your difficult emotions through and out of your body?

A Blessing for When They Have What Once Was Yours

When they have what you want
What once was yours
You want it back

Because never did you think
What you once both held
Would ever be only theirs

You don't want them to lose what they hold
But what would they feel like if they did?
Would they understand your torment?

When you wonder at the injustice of the world
When another holds what you've lost

Of course you want to
Scream
Ask why
And wish others could taste the bitterness of missing them

They were yours, after all

14

Grieving Secondary Losses

In the fall after Tyler's death, I took the kids to a friend's to go horseback riding. I was outside the corral fence, sitting in a tattered folding chair surrounded by almond hulls and dust. It was around 5:00 p.m. when I noticed the sun setting. It felt much earlier than usual. The warm day was quickly exchanged for a chilly evening as the sun dipped behind the barn. I felt a heaviness, as if someone was pushing down on my shoulders, as the sun set. A sense of dread swirled in my stomach at the thought of facing longer nights. Fall schedules had sent neighbors and friends indoors for school routines and early bedtimes, and I was feeling more alone.

A hint of woodsmoke drifted in the air, and I thought about how I couldn't wait for our first fire of the season. And then I remembered. I'd lost my fire builder. Tyler always had wood stacked by the back door and kept the fire going in our woodstove throughout the fall and winter seasons.

I didn't know all I had lost until I got there. When Tyler left for his fishing trip in June, the kids made him a Father's Day card, but he never made it home to see it. On Father's Day, I wasn't thinking about how we also lost our sparkler lighter and kid holder when they feared the blasts on the Fourth of July. I grieved Tyler in bits and pieces, and I never knew what we were going to miss until I got there.

So that early October night, I missed my fire builder. And something else. The way he looked at me across the room with the fire blazing. And the kids would just be doing kid stuff. And it didn't matter because when I looked at Tyler, and he looked at me, we said with unspoken delight, "Aren't they awesome?"

I lost the one who matched my enchantment with them. And I've never stopped missing that part of him.

When your loved one dies, you grieve their presence in your life, but soon you may notice other losses emerging. Those that follow your primary loss are called *secondary losses*. As you face losing your physical connection with your person, you may also notice the loss of companionship, familiar routines, plans for your future, finances, and your identity. Because secondary losses are often invisible to others, you may find it difficult to articulate the pain you are experiencing. Friends and family may not understand or acknowledge the enormity of the losses that follow your primary loss.

The Ripple Effect of Your Loss

Imagine tossing a heavy stone into a pond and watching the ripples reverberate from where it disappeared into the water. With grief, each ripple represents a facet of your loss. Because your loved one was an integral part of your everyday life, you have lost far more than just their physical presence.

The loss of your loved one, whether sudden or anticipated, often shatters your sense of self and security. Loss of physical safety, familiar routines, and hopes for your future shake your foundation. Loss of control, time, and purpose are just some aspects that contribute to your feelings of loss of self.

Your sense of belonging with others may be affected as you lose connections you and your loved one shared. For one mom, her person was no longer there to bring his unique presence to the dynamics of their mutual relationships. She noticed shifts in how she related to her friends and family, and how they, in turn, related to her. She said, "Without the presence of my husband, family gatherings fall flat. He was the life of the party, the one always making people laugh."

New Roles

When a person dies, there are significant changes in your daily routines and new roles to fill. For one mom, she missed the person she had coffee with each morning and the one she talked to at the end of her day. She said, "I miss the rhythms we shared, especially dinner and help with kids' bedtime routines. I feel the whole weight of my family now on my shoulders."

The loss of a partner often leaves voids that others can't fill. There are some roles you must assume in their absence, even when they are outside of your natural strengths or position in your family. Some may feel impossible to hold. You may long for your walking partner, your banker, your movie watcher, or the one who nurtured or wrestled with the kids. While you acknowledge your limitations, notice what is natural in your abilities. As your new roles evolve, there will be times when you strengthen your new muscles but also areas where you may need to find support.

In her book *Glitter and Glue*, author Kelly Corrigan introduces the concept of strengths each parent brings to their family.[1] The "glitter" parent is the fun parent who joins their child in play and embraces opportunities for spontaneity. The "glue" parent keeps the ship afloat. They tend to life's logistics by managing the calendar, signing permission slips, paying bills, and ensuring the uniform is washed for the game.

Your partner may have been strong in the areas you are not, and now you are left to hold both roles of glitter and glue. If you traditionally lean toward being the "glue" parent, putting the "glitter" into practice takes more intentionality. If you once shined as the "glitter" parent, it may take time to reorient to your family's newfound "glue" needs. One dad said, "I was always the 'fun dad,' and my wife was the organized one who kept us all on track. I'm learning new routines, but without her, it feels like we are living in chaos." Whether you naturally hold your family together with glue or throw glitter through levity and playfulness, know there is no right or wrong way to parent. You honor your love for your person when you open to your sorrow of their irreplaceableness.

Supporting Your Child

Your child will also experience secondary losses like changes in friendships, a decreased sense of security, and lost identity. One teen said, "I miss being known as the coach's son. I was proud of him, and he was proud of me. I miss him on the sidelines." For another teen, it meant losing the role model who guided them with needed mentoring. She said, "Losing my older sister meant I lost the one who I looked up to in my life."

Older children may think they must accept more responsibility. Your child may assume adult roles unnecessarily, resulting in overfunctioning with household responsibilities and care for their siblings. One mom shared, "At my husband's funeral, one of our relatives told my son, 'You're the man of the house now.' I jumped in and said, 'No, he isn't. He's still a child.'" She learned to remind her son that she didn't expect him to shoulder adult duties and communicated her plan to cover areas of need, adding, "I told him that he needs to remember to brush his teeth and do his homework, and I'll find ways to take care of the rest."

The death of a spouse or partner with the loss of their income brings financial strain. Medical bills or unexpected expenses contribute to these stressors. The loss of financial stability impacts your family's sense of security and may result in changes to your lifestyle. You may be forced to decide whether you can stay in your home, which could affect where your child goes to school. The loss of your child's home, teachers, or friends from school are secondary losses.

After the death of her husband, one mom longed to relocate closer to her parents. "I know that moving will give us more support, but my kids are worried about leaving their friends, and I'm worried that my decision will damage them in some way."

You can support your child by acknowledging secondary losses and inviting them to talk about the changes in their lives. Involve your child in these discussions when possible. Open the door to conversations and invite their voice when deciding who will do what duties and which roles need filling.

Grieving Your Loss over Time

The enormity of your loss will continue to reveal itself. Just as your relationship with your person would have grown and evolved, so will your grief as you enter new seasons of life without them. As one mom lamented, "I grieve his companionship and my dreams for my future with retirement plans, travel, and the hopes of enjoying grandchildren together someday." Another father mourned the rites of passage he wouldn't experience with his son, adding, "Teaching him to drive, his high school graduation, his entire future—I was robbed of it all."

Metabolizing the pain of secondary losses comes as you recognize and name *all* you lost when your person died. The death of your loved one was your primary loss, and all the losses that follow also require your attention.

Hand over heart, dear reader. Deep breath in.
Let it out. Say aloud, "I bring compassion to myself as
I honor all I've lost (name your secondary losses)."

HEALING PRACTICES

Reflection

1. Identify and write down the roles your person once carried in your family. Which ones do you now assume? Which feel impossible to fill? Who can fill one of these roles?
2. What secondary losses are you experiencing?
3. What secondary losses is your child experiencing?

Expressive Arts Invitation: What Is Lost and What Remains

Supplies needed: paper and markers or pencils

Some parts of our lives change or are lost when someone dies, while others stay the same. Talk with your child about the changes in your family. What roles did the person who died fill? And what secondary losses have they experienced? Brainstorm common changes in chores, who takes them to school, who makes dinner, friendships, bedtime routines, or childcare.

On the bottom of the paper, draw a hand that is closed, as if it's holding on to something. Draw balloons above the hand, and in them write or draw what remains or is still with you, even though the person died. For example, memories of your person, commonalities you share, and items that belonged to them. Draw strings to connect the balloons to the hand. Then draw more balloons and, on those, write or draw what you lost when your loved one died. Draw those strings but don't connect them to the hand, so what you lost floats to the sky.

Discussion Questions with Your Child

1. What balloon is the hardest to let go of for you?
2. What remaining balloons do you want to continue to hold?

A Blessing for the In-Between

In the liminal space
Between the hurt and the healing
The pain and the relief
May you find what you need

May assurance inhabit your weary days
May each breath renew your confidence

As you miss their company
Their help, their hands
May your frame be fortified

May rest be your friend
May you find them in your dreams

May the light of mercy be with you
To find your new way home

15

When Complexities Impact Grief

My mom died seven months after Tyler, and there were times I didn't think I would be okay. I lived with intense feelings of aloneness with no one in my inner circle who could relate to my experience with my mom's mental illness and death. I wanted to talk about her life and remember her with others like I did after Tyler died, but the trauma of the way she died overshadowed grieving who she was.

The shock and sadness of losing Tyler turned into overwhelming feelings of rejection, shame, and anger with my mom's death. I wondered if something was wrong with me; perhaps I was the common factor that brought tragedy to the world.

My bones felt fragile. Like I would crumble to the ground at the slightest touch.

I lived with unanswered questions, mental anguish, confusion, and guilt, wondering what more I could have done to save my mom. I also felt relieved that I was no longer living with the unpredictability of her mental health.

One morning, a year after my mom died, my best friend called and said she was in labor. She had asked me to be her support person in the delivery room, and I was excited to be with her. She labored and gave birth to her beautiful daughter, and then, like with most normal births, it took a few moments for the baby to find her first breaths. During those moments I held my own breath in terror. Because of trauma, I'd unknowingly adopted a narrative that believed I was the one causing calamity—and that if something terrible happened to this beautiful baby it would be because of me.

I've found ways to heal over the years as I've reformed my narratives and opened to the resources I need. And even as I bear the scars of living through the complexities of grief and trauma, I look back on all the ways I've healed and am healing.

I look back on all the ways I've healed and am healing, and I'm astounded at how a life can be restitched.

I f the death of your loved one overwhelmed your capacity to find what you needed to feel safe, complexities with trauma may influence your natural grief process. Numerous losses in a short span, the death of your child, death by violence, if your person's body was never recovered, suicide, an accident, or a natural disaster can all affect your healing. Lack of support and previous trauma can also increase complexities in your grief process. Your grief may also be compounded if you were part of the event that led to the death, like a car accident where you survived and your loved one didn't.

If Your Person Died by Suicide

If your person died by suicide, you face a grief process different from other deaths. In addition to your sadness and disbelief, you could experience a consuming sense of rejection, shame, confusion, and guilt. Even if you understand that your person was suffering from a mental illness and wanted to be out of pain, you may feel abandoned and wonder why they would leave you in this way. You may wonder if there was something else you could have done to save them. Or you fear judgment from others for the way your person died. Perhaps you feel relief if your person lived with a mental illness that resulted in unpredictable or unsafe behavior. Remember that in grief, you often hold conflicting emotions at the same time.

Because of the sudden and sometimes violent nature of suicide, you may replay the final moments as your brain works to understand the death. Our brains are good at creating narratives to help us find what we need to heal. Asking why and what-if questions is a natural part of our search for answers.

Grieving a suicide death often disrupts families because each person may have a different idea on how to talk about the death. Some may want to keep the details private, and others may want to talk openly. One dad said, "I feel like there is a lot of denial in our family about the gravity of my wife's mental illness. I want to talk openly about her death, but not everyone is comfortable with talking about how she died."

Religious communities may view suicide as a sin, some even teaching that if someone dies of suicide, they won't go to heaven. These views on those who die from the pain of depression increase feelings of shame and stigma for those grieving their death. One mom said, "After my daughter died of suicide, I wondered if she was in heaven. But then I thought of God welcoming her early, just like I would do if she showed up a day early to Thanksgiving." She added, "I know God welcomed her with compassion for the mental suffering she endured on earth."

If Your Person Died by Homicide

Homicide is another death that is complex to grieve. Because a death by murder is often more public than other deaths, you are likely affected by the added stressors of media and public attention. You and your family are stripped of the private space needed to grieve.

Your grief process may be delayed because your energy is invested in bringing the perpetrator to justice. The intensity of court hearings and ongoing trials adds another layer of distress to your loss.

The shock of being robbed of your loved one at the hands of someone else and the mental anguish of knowing the physical violence they endured batter you with feelings of helplessness and devastation. You could be flooded by a cascade of mental images of the death. You are suddenly thrown into investigations, delaying your needed mourning. Many times, viewing and touching your loved one's body isn't possible because it is part of the evidence, further complicating your grief process.

Because of the time trials take, you don't have a chance to mourn the death like you would without those surrounding obstacles. The time of waiting for the outcome is especially distressing and victimizes you and your family continually with testimonies and images. One mom shared her feelings of uncertainty about attending the trial. "I can't decide if I should go or if I have what it takes to testify." Each family member may have differing opinions on how involved they want to be in court proceedings. As one dad voiced, "I needed to know everything about what happened to my son while my wife wanted to be spared of the details."

Knowing what happened when your person died helps you process the death; however, if your loved one's case is unsolved, you are left waiting for answers. As one mom said, "I feel like I can't move on. I need to see justice served." Another dad mentioned, "Our daughter's murder is a cold case now, and we're left with no answers. All her belongings are in evidence. At the very least, we wanted her cell phone, with her photos and conversations with friends and family."

You may be advised to forgive the perpetrator because it's the "right thing to do." This kind of "forgiveness" can lead to harmful, reductive, all-or-nothing thinking that you must choose either mercy or vengeance. Remember, you can hold conflicting emotions at the same time, and rage is a common reaction after a loved one dies from homicide. It fuels your survival. One mom said, "As I healed after our son's murder, I sensed a lightening of the consuming bitterness that kept me from living the life I wanted. Over time, I found I could hold my healing alongside my rage from all that has been taken from us." Trust your inner wisdom if it feels like pressure to forgive will compromise your genuine healing. Premature forgiveness before fully processing your pain represses the growth needed for transformation, leading to resentment.

If Your Person Died by Substance Use

If your person died by substance use, such as an accidental overdose or fentanyl poisoning, you are facing a complex loss. They may have used substances occasionally in social ways, had a substance use illness, or died from a single-use dose. If they lived with the illness of addiction, you might have anticipatorily grieved long before your person died, and you may hold feelings of longing for them alongside relief. You may wish your relationship was different and grieve the life you hoped for them and your family.

Losing a loved one through substance use is often compounded by feelings of guilt and anger along with sadness. Your rage may be directed toward your loved one, the friends they were influenced by, or their dealer. One mom acknowledged feelings of anger toward her son. "He knew using drugs was destroying his body, and we all supported him in getting sober. I am devastated that he started using again."

One mom shared conflicting feelings about how much to tell her young children. "Their dad was the most playful with the kids when he was using, and they still talk about what a fun dad he was. I want them to know the truth about his substance use but don't want to ruin the image they have of him."

You may wonder what else you could have done to prevent the death of your loved one or to support their recovery, even when you know it was out of your control. If you lack others in your life who bring compassion and understanding about the illness of substance use, you may feel especially alone.

Disenfranchised Grief

Disenfranchised grief is when you can't openly acknowledge or publicly grieve your person's death due to the nature of your relationship with them or judgment from others. Grief that is disenfranchised complicates your mourning.

You may feel the nature of your relationship with them when they died dictates your permission to grieve. "We had been divorced for a few years," one mom commented, "but I'm still mourning my ex's death—all that we shared with our history and especially what my children have lost." One young adult struggled with conflicting feelings after learning her biological mother had died: "She was never active in my life, but she is still a part of me. My friends don't understand why I'm grieving for someone I never really knew. Her death ended my dream of having a relationship with her someday."

Other times, your grief can be disenfranchised when it is met with judgment or a lack of remorse from others, like if your person's own actions led to their death. Physical altercations, driving while under the influence, recklessness, death by substance use, or suicide are all deaths that could incur judgment. The way your person died and any responsibility they had in their death does not negate your need to mourn or their value.

Supporting Your Child

Children bereaved by a stigmatized death through suicide, violence, or substance use can also experience a more complicated grief process. Your child may have more feelings of shame, rage, and fear. After a homicide, your child may have fears about more violence against themselves or someone they love. Feelings of wanting to harm the person who caused the death are common. When you model openness about how the person died and use clear language, you provide an environment where your child can ask questions and talk openly about how they feel when discussing the death with you and others.

After a death by substance use, your child may fear the death of other family or friends who are currently using. Explain to your child that substance use is an illness, but it's not a sickness they can catch, such as a cold or the flu. If the substance use death was caused by a substance use illness, it may be hard to remember the person before their addiction. Sharing memories about the person who died and remembering their attributes aside from their addiction can help you grieve all their parts, not just the part of them with an illness.

Explain to your child that someone who dies by suicide often lives with a mental illness that affects their brain function and influences their choice to end their life. Your child might wonder if they or someone else in their family will live with mental illness and die in a similar way. They may also be concerned about your or their siblings' health and safety. Provide reassurance by communicating what you are doing to keep yourself and their siblings healthy and safe.

When there are unknown details surrounding the death, you likely have unanswered questions. If your child asks why the death happened and you don't know, you can respond with, "I don't know, but I wish I knew." If your child wonders if there was anything they could have done to prevent their loved one from dying, reassure them that their words or thoughts can't cause a person's body to stop working. As hard as it may be to have these conversations with your child, think of it as the beginning of the ongoing trust-building you'll have with them as they grow. You are beginning the process by helping your child understand the cause of the death, and you can provide more details as they become available and as your child's understanding matures.[1]

Because of the stigma attached to deaths by homicide, suicide, and substance use, consider preparing your child for any unhelpful or hurtful comments they may receive. You could say, "Some people haven't experienced the death of a loved one like our family has, and so they can't understand what we're going through. They may be judgmental or say unkind words. You can always talk to me." To prepare your child for prying questions they may receive from others, help them decide how they wish to answer. You can say, "Some people are very curious about how someone died, and they may ask you questions. You can decide what questions, if any, you want to answer."

If the person who died caused harm to themselves or others, your child may experience shame because they are related to them. One child voiced, "When people make comments about my dad's 'bad choices,' it makes me wonder if that means I'm 'bad' too."

Exploring Your Healing

If your grief makes it difficult for you or your child to function in daily life, find a qualified mental health professional. Traumatic grief responds well to professional and social support. In addition to individual counseling, look for a group with those affected by a traumatic death to support you. In his book *The Body Keeps the Score*, physician and trauma researcher Bessel van der Kolk says, "Being able to feel safe with other people is probably the single most important aspect of mental health; safe connections are fundamental to meaningful and satisfying lives."[2]

Because trauma is experienced in a sensory way, sensations can get stuck in your body. When faced with a similar sensory experience, like smells or images, you may feel like you are experiencing your trauma in the present moment. When your grief is complex, you may have chronic, suppressed, or delayed reactions. Find ways to connect with and express your emotions through your body. Yoga, for example, can help you feel more empowered through a sense of safety and well-being through focused breathing, grounding, and increasing awareness.

Self-compassion is another way to heal when grief is complicated, and it can remind you that you are human. When you notice you are blaming or criticizing yourself, you can use mindful breathing to bring yourself back to the present moment. Feel your breath where it enters and exits your body. Notice the sensations in the back of your nose and throat as you breathe. You can then use thought-stopping techniques such as imagining your critical thoughts as bubbles and popping them in the air by clapping your hands.

Engaging with bilateral movements, which cross the midline of your body, can help your brain and body connect. Swaying from side to side, swimming, walking, cycling, playing tennis or Ping-Pong, dancing, or scribbling with both hands at the same time stimulates both hemispheres of your brain, promoting a sense of control, emotional regulation, and calm.[3]

A sense of safety is key to healing when grief is complicated. As you grieve your loss in bits and pieces, do so in a way that honors your need for safety at the pace that's right for you. You need physical, mental, and emotional support as you integrate your experience and find ways to heal. Continue to connect with others who can validate your experience.

Hand over heart, dear reader. Deep breath in.
Let it out. Say aloud, "I give myself the
compassion I need as I find safe ways to heal."

HEALING PRACTICES

Reflection

1. What healing practices help you feel better when you are overwhelmed with the complexities of grief?
2. What else would you like to build into your healing practices?

Expressive Arts Invitation: My Iceberg

Supplies needed: paper and crayons, colored pencils, markers, watercolors, or oil pastels

There are parts of your grief that many people know and some only your close friends or family know. There may even be aspects about your grief that no one else knows. It helps to talk to someone you trust about what you wish others knew about your grief. In nature, if too much pressure is placed on an iceberg, it can flip over, causing a tidal wave. When you don't express your emotions to others, your iceberg can flip too.

Draw an iceberg with one part above the water and two parts below, so it has three layers and two are under the water's surface. On the tip of the iceberg, above the water line, write the feelings you show others. Under the surface, in the middle of your iceberg, write what very few people know about your grief. On the bottom of the iceberg, write what you haven't shared with others about how you feel. These are emotions that may be hard for you to express. Use colors that represent your grief emotions to shade in the iceberg.

Discussion Questions with Your Child

1. What parts of your grief are easy to show to others?
2. What parts of your grief are more difficult for you to express?
3. What helps you to share the hidden parts of your grief?

A Blessing for When Grief Is Complicated

May you know
What hurt you today
Won't always assault you

May your shattered heart find its way
May the chasm that is left
Be a remnant that says, "They were here"
They will always be

May others remind you when you forget
They were real
And they were yours

When your soul is weary
Your ragged edges unfurling
When the "if onlys" are an encore
Hold tight

May your splintered heart be held
For good

16

Enlarging Your Soul

One morning, several months after Tyler's accident, I was standing in the kitchen, listening to a radio talk show where one of the guests had a story that matched mine. Her husband and his friends had died in a plane crash. I remember listening while standing still for a long time, feeling a flutter of relief and an expectancy that I would survive.

It was my first spark of wondering if maybe I could help someone else someday.

I held on to a verse in the Bible that says, "He comes alongside us when we go through hard times, and before you know it, he brings us alongside someone else who is going through hard times so that we can be there for that person just as God was there for us" (2 Cor. 1:4 MSG).

A few weeks later, a woman from the cemetery came to my home with a binder of grave markers to select for Tyler's grave. We sat together at my kitchen table as I leafed through the pages, trying to find one that fit him. She casually mentioned that her husband had also died a few years before. I didn't know any other widows then, so I looked up from the page and noticed how okay she was. Seeing someone whose face was full of life held promise.

As the darkness crept in over the following months and years, I knew there was no way around it. I had to let it in. Letting the darkness in

meant getting through sleepless nights and days feeling fragile and afraid.
But I was learning to trust that I would not always feel the way I did in
moments of despair.

I noticed a profound empathy for those grieving that I didn't have
before Tyler died. And I hoped perhaps one day I would be the one sit-
ting across the table.

I wondered what it would be like to reach out and take the hand of
someone facing the unimaginable.

And I learned to live in what can't be fixed.

As you are with your grief, you may notice there are times
you feel despair. The word *despair* comes from the Latin
word *sperare*, which surprisingly means, "To hope, expect." Yet feeling despair is often when hope seems out of reach.

Brené Brown says, "We run from grief because loss scares us,
yet our hearts reach toward grief because the broken parts want to
mend."[1] Like the buffalo that survives the storm by walking into it
instead of away, there is a gentle invitation to encounter our loss and
make room for uncomfortable emotions. The work of grief is to honestly express, revisit memories, and mourn what is physically gone.

Even with a butterfly, metamorphosis only happens inside the
dark cocoon. What if the caterpillar broke out too soon? It would
never strengthen its wings enough to fly. Finding new life means
gently encountering the darkness.

Despair is not a place you want to be. It's certainly not a place
our culture finds comfortable. Yet being with your suffering at a pace
that feels right for you creates room for wisdom, empathy, strength,
and meaning. Elisabeth Kübler-Ross writes,

> The most beautiful people we have known are those who have
> known defeat, known suffering, known struggle, known loss, and
> have found their way out of the depths. These persons have an ap-
> preciation, a sensitivity, and an understanding of life that fills them

with compassion, gentleness, and a deep loving concern. Beautiful people do not just happen.[2]

Over time, you may notice a softening of the sharpness of your grief that moves to an expansion of your capacity. Perhaps you were overwhelmed by social interactions after the loss but are now engaging in more extended conversations. Or your sleep might be improving. Maybe the images in your mind from the death are diminishing, or the guilt doesn't feel as severe as it once did.

You may have noticed your inner light seemed muted after the death but now is beginning to shine a bit brighter. We all have a spark within us that dims during our suffering and then burns brighter as we heal. One dad described it like this: "When my wife died, I lost my laugh. I didn't feel like the person I once was. It took time for parts of me to reemerge and grow." Trusting your spark will return is holding an expectancy of good for your future.

Psychiatrist Viktor Frankl was a survivor of a Nazi concentration camp. As he studied the suffering of other Holocaust survivors, he discovered how humans create meaning as they search for purpose in their pain. In his book *Man's Search for Meaning*, he noticed that searching for meaning relates to resilience, and suffering can increase our capacity for not only sorrow but joy.[3] Going through difficult life experiences can promote resilience in the face of new challenges, although these are muscles you never wanted to build.

As your soul enlarges, you may experience more strength, a widening capacity to love and be loved, a more profound peace, and greater joy. And remember, like the opposing forces of weather, the sun and rain can coexist. In the well-known words of Albert Camus, "In the middle of winter I at last discovered that there was in me an invincible summer."[4]

Hope doesn't need to match the scale of your loss. If you think of hope as an anchor, you will see that the anchor never matches the size of the boat. Often, little glimmers of hope will support you to your next moment. Gazing at your child's hands, receiving a friend's text at the right time, watching a sunrise, holding a warm coffee cup, or feeling the waft of an afternoon breeze can help you through your day.

Making Meaning

For some, making meaning out of suffering communicates their desire to transcend the tragedies of the world. You may resonate with this desire for transcendence and wish to find or make meaning from your loss. Or maybe you don't. It's understandable if you feel it's impossible to make meaning out of something so tragic. Only you can know what feels genuine for you.

You don't need to try to make sense of your loss during this time. One dad said, "I am not interested in my loss being a source of self-improvement. Just surviving each day feels like a win." Or you may find your loss changes your lens in some ways. Another dad shared, "After my wife died, I felt a new sense of courage. I wanted to make more out of life's moments because I've learned it can change." In time, you will find your cadence of healing rhythms. Where once there was constant sorrow, you may notice shimmers of light. The laugh you thought you lost returns in some small way, and you notice you are finding your way home to the person you are becoming.

Post-Traumatic Growth

Researchers Richard Tedeschi and Lawrence Calhoun found that transformative and positive changes can happen after trauma. They identified five possible areas of growth: personal strength, a deeper relatability to others, an openness to new possibilities, a greater appreciation for life, and spiritual growth after tragedy. "Service to others seems to be a hallmark of this growth process," Tedeschi says. "Part of the process that leads to a meaningful life involves something that has an impact, something that matters, and that usually involves other people." Tedeschi and Calhoun stress the importance of support from close friends, family, and mental health professionals after trauma and how that relates to how well a person will fare.[5]

You may notice increased compassion or a deepening of your faith as you move through your loss. Finding support, adopting strong coping skills, and developing the ability to express your grief promote this type of growth. Embodied expression helps connect your body, mind, and soul to joy, mastery, empathy, playfulness, and curiosity. You begin to understand what you need as you and your family experience small moments of restorative connection.

Another transformative change for children who receive the support they need after a death is a desire to explore helping fields when considering their future careers. One teen at Jessica's House who had group and family support after her dad died when she was four is now in college studying applied psychology and dreams of expanding grief support access to children. "Going to Jessica's House helped me express the grief I was experiencing. I was able to mourn through art, music, and play. It was a unique experience in that I was sitting in a room with other kids going through the same loss. I wasn't alone."

Supporting Your Child

Your support for your child as they lean into their grief increases their capacity to hold both the darkness and the light. Their feelings of grief may intensify at times, but they are learning to move through each moment.

The most important long-term protective factor for your child's mental health is having a warm and loving relationship with a trusted adult.[6] Having a parent or caregiver who is supportive helps children build resilience after a stressful childhood experience. Quality friendships and peer support help your child feel connected and more competent. Feeling part of a "bigger purpose" can also be a protective factor for a child. Cultivating a sense of spirituality can promote resiliency by broadening your child's view of their current circumstances and providing supportive, long-term, intergenerational relationships.

Your Sacred Story

As time passes, big and small life events will ignite missing your loved one. Some families say that the intensity of their grief bursts have lessened over time. One mom said, "The force of my longing for my son eased over time. I'm finding room for love alongside my pain. As the years go by, I notice that my grief doesn't sting in quite the same way." There is no closure in grief but rather an opening to what remains and what could be.

When a storm alters a landscape, nature finds ways to renew. As you find ways to heal, you transform the landscape of your life and family. Your presence and care for your child will strengthen and stabilize them for all their tomorrows. Indeed, your grief will never end because your love never ends. You metabolize your loss over time, and it becomes your sacred story.

Thank you for being here, dear reader. Hand over heart. Deep breath in. Let it out. Say aloud, "I bring compassion to myself as I trust in my capacity to heal."

HEALING PRACTICES

Reflection

1. If you could go back to when the death first happened, what would you tell yourself based on what you know now?
2. What strengths are you noticing that you want to carry forward?

Expressive Arts Invitation: Time Machine

Supplies needed: paper and pencils, markers, colored pencils, or crayons

Ask your child to draw a picture of a time machine with three doors.

In a door marked "Past," invite them to write or draw what they miss about their loved one, what they wish they would have said, and a regret they have—what they wish they didn't say or do and what they want to leave in the past.

In a door marked "Present," invite them to draw or write a person who is helping them now and an activity that brings them strength.

In a door marked "Future," invite them to draw or write what they want to tell their loved one and their wishes, hopes, and dreams for their future.

Discussion Questions with Your Child

1. What from your "Past" door do you most want to close and leave behind?
2. Who or what from your "Present" door is helping you the most right now?
3. What are you hopeful for in your "Future" door?

Discover Resilience

During this season of healing, you can discover resilience through

Connections—finding your connections with those who make you feel safe and loved.

Coping—practicing coping skills like breath work, yoga, and power poses.

Culture—honoring your personal beliefs and values.

Clarity—finding your way through praying, writing, and having a sacred listener such as a friend or counselor.

Creating—expressing yourself through art, poetry, writing, music, and being in nature.

Compassion—being tender to yourself in your thoughts, words, and actions.

A Blessing for Enlarging Your Soul

May you feel the sun
Even when it's not shining

May the warmth of it thaw the earth
So that which is born in darkness
Will yield itself to the life-giver

And as new life emerges
May it carry within it what has been
To behold what is old and new
And carry forth a blossom

May the blossom mature as fruit
May it nourish your soul
In what remains
And what will be

A BENEDICTION

I am sitting in front of my Christmas tree on my fifth Christmas without Carter, thinking, I don't hate Christmas this year. My wonder is returning as I notice small splendors of the season. Our family isn't what it once was, but the shards are returning from the earth, taking a form. It's not the same, but there are corners and edges, and we are stitching the inside back together through surrender, mercy, and grace.

———————

Thank you for inviting us to be part of your healing. We didn't want to meet this way, but being your companion is an honor. Colleen and I have held you in our hearts and minds these past several months as we've written these words for you. We hope to hear your story someday. I've imagined you sitting in a chair across from me as I've sat in the same spot each dark morning thinking of you, fingers on laptop keys. I've watched the sunrise as I breathed for you, praying for you to be birthed into a wider circle of healing. Asking for a spark to light your way to your next moment.

I want to thank Colleen for writing this book with me. When I interviewed her for Jessica's House, I asked her to tell me a life accomplishment she was proud of, and she said, "Being published." At the same time, I was working on a book concept. The first week she was with Jessica's House, I called her as I drove down the hill from a writers' conference at Mount Hermon and asked if she would write a book with me. What a gift to write this book together. I treasure every moment we've had on this project. Who knew we could have fun writing a grief book?

We want to thank all those who believed in this project. Our beloved agent, Wendy, our acquiring editor, Rebekah, our developmental editor, Jamie, and the entire Baker Books team.

We are grateful for our faithful Jessica's House staff, interns, and volunteers who read and gave valued feedback on our manuscript, along with beloved family and friends.

To Donna Schuurman, director emeritus of the Dougy Center, the first bereavement center for families in the United States, thank you for your mentorship and contributions to our manuscript. Your fierce advocacy for children and families who are grieving is our aspiration.

To Linda Stuhmer from EMC Health, Inc., and Jeffrey Lewis from Legacy Health Endowment, thank you for believing in this project and for your dedicated resources, leadership, and unwavering support.

To our husbands who held home responsibilities while we disappeared to write, having your loving encouragement and understanding pushed us to the finish line. To those who have gone before us—our hearts long for you. And to our children, family, and friends, our community of support who championed us through this project, we love you forever.

To the families of Jessica's House, your healing is our inspiration. May you be held.

Always,
Erin and Colleen

FURTHER RESOURCES

SUPPORTING YOUR CHILD (AGES 0–12)

Babies and Toddlers (Ages 0–2)

Your baby or toddler may not understand the concept of death but may notice when someone significant is missing from their environment. They don't have the language to express their emotions after the loss of a parent or sibling.

You may notice increased crying, searching for the person who died, visible anxiety, trouble sleeping, less interest in play or eating, or regression in development. Your child's movements may be slower or more active than usual. They may have difficulty with self-soothing and take longer to comfort.

You can help your baby or toddler by keeping to routines as much as possible. Repeat reading their favorite story and sing familiar songs. Play music and sway together to release the energy of grief. It also helps to create a quiet space where your toddler can access comforting items like their favorite toys or blankets. Your physical presence and touch support their sense of safety.

Preschoolers (Ages 3–4)

Children at this age begin noticing death in the natural world, such as bugs, animals, flowers, or birds, but they don't understand death's permanence. They often ask where their loved one is and when they will return. They may have magical thinking where they believe they can somehow bring their person back.

Young children may be candid and say to others, "My daddy died," as they process and state their reality. Your reflection of, "Yes, your daddy died," creates a welcoming space for them to express themselves without reservation.

You may notice your preschooler crying more often or expressing feelings of anxiety or fear. They may look or ask for the person who died and express intense emotions that feel disruptive to the family environment, like screaming or hitting. You can follow up with any behavior you notice. For example, "It's okay to feel mad, but I won't let you hit someone." Honoring your family values of not hurting others even when you're mad creates a sense of safety for children who are grieving.

When you feel dysregulated in your grief, your child's intense displays of emotions can overwhelm you. You may need to take a moment to come back to your body. Look at your hands, feel your feet on the floor, press your hand over your heart, and take a breath. Look around the room and notice something calming in your environment. When you feel more at ease, sit by your child and be with them in their feelings.

Children can feel insecure with life changes at this age, so consistent reassurance from parents and other trusted adults reinforces their sense of safety. Keeping routines and schedules also provides security. Offer choices when possible—Would they like to take a bath before or after dinner? Do they want to wear a dress or pants today? During a time when safety has been stripped away, making a choice gives your child a sense of control.

Provide opportunities for creative play as an outlet for your child to process their experience. Medical kits, dollhouses, and rescue vehicles can help them play out what they imagine happened to their person or what they witnessed. Play helps children process their grief as they explore their world and how they relate to it.

Keeping art supplies available can help them express through art as needed. Mirroring them by engaging with their play helps their grief be witnessed. One way to help your child feel seen during play is through sportscasting, which is when you narrate what you see them doing: "I see you looking at the fire truck. Now you're picking it up," or "I notice you are drawing with a purple crayon. Now you're drawing a line."

Elementary School (Ages 5–12)

Your child is forming their understanding of death's permanence during this time. Like at the preschool age, they may wonder if death is temporary or if there is something they can do to bring the person back. They may feel they somehow caused the death. Continue to talk about the death and how the person died to remind them of the truth about what happened.

Keep routines as much as possible. You can support your child by discussing who will care for them when you aren't there. Touch, hugs, and physical assurance can help them regulate their emotions. You may notice your child becomes more anxious about their own health and safety or yours. You can assure them that what happened is relatively rare, and you are doing everything you can to keep them and yourself healthy and safe. Reassure your child that there will always be someone to take care of them by sharing your plan of who they would live with if something happened to you.

Your child may naturally be interested in how their person died and ask questions about the person's body and what happens after death. It's okay to admit what you don't know as you share your beliefs with them. You can say, "I believe your daddy is in heaven, but I wish he was here with us, and I'm wondering what heaven is like."

Your child may try to hide their emotions to protect you. Explain that it's natural to be sad after someone dies, and their tears represent their love for their person and how much they miss them. It's also common for children not to cry. Normalizing not crying, or not being able to cry, along with emotions like relief and anger, helps them feel understood.

As your child matures, their comprehension of death expands, deepening their understanding of what they lost. It's natural for children to experience intense emotions as they re-grieve the loss amid new life stages, accomplishments, and transitions. Help your child feel connected to their loved one by ceremonially remembering them during developmental milestones.

How to Talk about Death

Your child is seeking answers for how their person died and may be curious about the details surrounding the death. Answering your child's questions in a clear and concrete manner helps them build a framework around what occurred, grounding them in the truth of what happened.

Using words like *lost* or *passed* causes confusion. Using simple and concrete language when explaining death by using the word *died* helps your child understand what happened. Let your child's questions guide your conversation to prevent sharing more than they're ready for in that moment. Assure them they can always come to you with their questions. You can start by asking, "I'm wondering what you're wondering." If you don't know an answer, you can say, "I don't know, but I will try to find the answer."

When explaining your loved one's death to your child, use simple language to help them understand what happened. You can say, "I have something very hard to tell you. Your dad had a heart attack, which caused his body to stop working, and he died," or "I have something very hard to tell you. Your mom was in a car accident. The accident hurt her body so badly that it stopped working and she died."

For a homicide death, you can explain, "I have something very hard to tell you. Your mom died. Someone made her body stop working _____ (by a gun, with a knife). This is called a homicide, or murder."

For a suicide death, you can explain, "I have something very hard to tell you. Your dad made his own body stop working _____ (with a gun, with a rope) and he died. This is called suicide."

For a substance use death, you can explain, "I have something very hard to tell you. Your mom used a substance that made her body stop working. She died from a substance use illness."

Across Age Groups

After the death, your child may return to behaviors they once relied on when they were younger. This can look like fits of anger and protest or wanting to sleep next to you. They may also revert to thumb-sucking or baby talk to re-create a time when they felt safe. Grief expression, play, routines, and structure bring your child safety and help them as they heal and return to typical developmental behaviors.[1]

Your child may also have questions about burial and cremation. You may want to share your family's traditions and beliefs about the body and where the person's soul lives now and ask your child what questions they may have. Remind them that when someone dies, they don't feel pain anymore because their body stopped working. Ask them what questions they have about burial or cremation. Explain that cremation is when a person's body is put in a box, then placed in a very hot chamber. The heat in the chamber turns the body into ashes. The ashes feel and look like sand. Their loved one's ashes are then placed in a container like a box or a special vase called an urn. These ashes are called remains, and they can be kept in the special container, buried, or scattered outside in a place that is special for them. If their loved one is buried, explain that their body is placed in a box called a casket. The casket is put into a concrete container in the ground at a cemetery, and dirt is placed on top. Their loved one's name and the dates when they were born and died are written on a marker, sometimes called a headstone, that is placed on the ground above the casket.

Remind your child that the cemetery or ash scattering site is a place they may want to visit. Discuss visiting the location and talk about ideas on what they would like to do if they go, like bringing flowers, a picture, or a letter.

Allow your child to teach you what they need to feel supported in their grief. Some days, supporting your child may feel impossible as you carry your own grief. As you take care of yourself, remember that your presence and connection are the greatest gifts you can give your child right now.

SUPPORTING YOUR TEEN (AGES 13–19)

A
t this age, your teen can grasp the concept of death and know it is irreversible. The death of your loved one could be the first time your teen encounters loss and may call into question your teen's previous beliefs that they are invincible.

Because your teen is preparing to live in a peer world, they will naturally be concerned about their friends' reaction to their loss. Teens often feel misunderstood by peers who haven't experienced a death like they have. Because grief affects how they move from dependence to independence, they may be worried about their friends' responses to the death, feel embarrassed because of the attention drawn to them after the loss, have drastic mood swings, and depend more on their peers than family for support during this time.

Adolescence is already a challenging time in development with rapid changes in their physical body. Your teen is also experiencing a vital time of identity shaping. They are discovering their individuality apart from their role within their family unit. They may be exploring their beliefs on what happens after someone dies and their own faith.

The death of their loved one shifts their place within your family. If they are the oldest and their parent died, they may wonder if they need to assume an adult role for younger siblings. They may feel like they need to care for you or take on more household or financial responsibilities. When the death of a sibling alters their birth order lineup, the changes might mean they are now the only living child, the youngest child, or the oldest child in the home.

Your teen may find it difficult to express their emotions. They may use humor to mask their feelings and feel alone if they don't know other teens who have experienced a similar death. Teens often find the intensity of their emotions overwhelming and look for ways to disengage. You might notice they need more personal space. Watch for withdrawal that turns to isolation, or risky behavior.

At times, you may notice your teen returning to younger behaviors such as angry outbursts or wanting to sleep next to you. You can support their need for connection as they seek feelings of comfort and safety. Trust they'll know when they no longer need your support in these ways and take their lead as they find what they need.

Your teen may shield you from their emotions and make it appear as though they are okay as a way of protecting you. You can't force your teen to talk, but you can be curious about what interests them. Discuss subjects other than grief and move to topics about your shared loss as you sense an opening. To feel, heal, and express their emotions, your teen needs to have a felt sense of safety. Easing in with questions such as "If you could ask Dad a question right now, what would it be?" or "What is the best advice Mom gave you?" can generate conversation around memories, which might feel less threatening than talking about their feelings. Reflect on other trusted adults like teachers, coaches, close friends, or family members who might reach out to your teen to offer opportunities for connection and support. These times of connection provide a space for your teen to process thoughts and feelings with you or other safe adults.

Explaining Death to Your Teen

You can support your teen by being honest about the circumstances of the death. Include them in age-appropriate discussions and be available to answer their questions. Let your teen's questions guide your conversation to prevent sharing more than they're ready to hear in that moment. Assure them they can always come to you with their questions. If you don't know an answer, you can say, "I don't know, but I will try to find the answer." The way someone died is a matter of public record, and you build trust with your teen when they learn the truth from you instead of others.

Examples of how to explain the death to your teen include: "I have something very hard to tell you. Your dad had a heart attack and he died," or "I have something very hard to tell you. Your mom was in a car accident. There were a lot of injuries to her body, and she died."

For a homicide death, you can explain, "I have something very hard to tell you. Your mom died by homicide. Someone ended her life by _____."

For a suicide death, you can explain, "I have something very hard to tell you. Your dad died by suicide. He ended his own life by _____."

For a substance use death, you can explain, "I have something very hard to tell you. Your dad died from a substance use illness. He used a substance that caused his body to stop working."

Supporting Your Teen

As you model mourning by outwardly expressing your emotions through crying and talking about what you're feeling, you give your teen permission to mourn. As you encourage the uniqueness of their grief and how it differs from yours, you validate their feelings and opinions and affirm how each person in a family grieves differently.

Teens often find comfort and familiarity in routine, so keep your family rhythms as best you can. Consistency helps them know what to expect next. Offer choices as often as possible: "Would you like to do your homework after school or after dinner?" You can ask them, "What sounds good for dinner?" and let them choose. Giving your teen choices empowers them during a time when their sense of control is shattered.

If their parent died, talk about the plan you have in place for who they would live with if you were to die. This may feel like a hard conversation, but teens often think about what will happen to them if their other parent dies. They need the reassurance that they'll be in good care if something happens to you.

Give your teen opportunities for fun, time with friends, rest, and physical activity. Honor the energy of their grief and make space for what they need to express. Provide them with outlets for connections with peers and space to disengage through time alone. Your teen may need to move excess energy out of their body through physical activity outside. Consider taking a walk with them or playing a game of catch. Or perhaps they're exhausted, and watching a movie or taking a nap is what they need.

As your teen matures, they will experience changes in their grief. Big milestones and small moments may illuminate how much they miss their loved one. During grief bursts, acknowledge your teen's feelings by reflecting their words, and affirm their feelings by saying, "You wish your dad were here; so do I." You can ask them, "What do you need right now?" as they process their emotions.

You don't need to have all the answers to support your teen. When you feel overwhelmed, remind yourself that being open to their grief helps them heal. You don't need to take away their pain. You can simply be in your pain together at a pace that feels right for both of you. You are both finding your way, individually and together.

EQUIPPING YOUR COMMUNITY TO SUPPORT YOU

For Your Friends and Family

Your friends and family may want to help but not know what to do or say during this time. The following section is a guide you can share with those who want to support you. You can find a shareable version by visiting JessicasHouse.org.

How to Be a Companion

When someone you care about is grieving, knowing how to support them isn't easy. You may feel helpless and wish you could take away their pain. Even those of us who work with families in grief every day have no solutions to the pain of grief. You can't change what happened, but you can create a safe space where transformation and healing emerge.

Because each person's grief is unique, allow your friend to teach you what is helpful for them. Their grief may change from day to day. One day they may want to go out, and the next stay in. One day they may want someone to be with them, and another day be alone.

181

You can take the guesswork out of helping your friend by simply reflecting what you see and hear. If they are crying, it's okay to cry with them. If they are quiet, be in silence with them. If they are reminiscing, join them in their memories. If they laugh at a funny story, laugh along and share the moment. Mirroring a griever's energy is the best way to create a space where they can heal.

Lean into your natural abilities in the support you offer. As you and others surround your friend who is grieving, you each offer a unique way of supporting them.

If you enjoy gift giving, send a gift card for groceries or a meal delivery service. Donate in their loved one's memory or send a gift card from a nursery to choose a tree that can be planted. Practical gifts like a home-cooked meal, dinners for the freezer, disposable plates and cutlery, groceries, snacks for the kids, or essentials like toilet paper and toothpaste are often helpful. You could also gift comforting items like a journal and pen, a weighted blanket, or a robe.

If acts of service fit your strengths, put your love into action by baking them cookies, offering to run errands, or asking if you can drive them to doctor's appointments. Help with repairs around the house such as replacing light bulbs, cleaning gutters, repairing fences, or doing car maintenance. Take their dirty laundry home and return it clean and folded. Mow their lawn, weed their garden, or take their garbage cans to the road. Offer to care for their pets, including feeding and cleaning up after them, walking them, and taking them to the vet. Gather the mail or send a housekeeper.

Instead of saying, "Let me know if you need anything," offer concrete help by asking, "I'm running to the store right now, what can I pick up for you?" Or say, "I'd like to drop dinner off this week. Please let me know if tonight or tomorrow night is better for you."

For their kids, offer to pick them up from school, help with homework, take them to sports practice or music lessons, or make school lunches. Say, "I would love to spend time with your kids this afternoon so you can rest." Bring a bag of children's books and read to them. Take them to ice cream, a movie, or the park.

You could also come alongside your friend or family member with a project—they may want to clean out a closet or the garage, plant a garden, or start a new hobby. Sharing an activity is one way to make meaningful connections and spend time together.

If you prefer expressing your love through words, send voice-mails, direct messages, cards, and letters. Text them photos of their loved one with your favorite memories. If you text or call, remind them they don't need to respond. Some words and phrases that communicate your support are, "I'll always remember _____ (share a memory)," "My love and support surround you," "I thought of _____ (loved one's name) when I saw _____ today," "I've been thinking about _____ (loved one's name) and how they impacted me by _____ (share a way they touched your life)," "You're getting through breath by breath, and I'm with you," "I'll never forget their _____ (smile, kindness, how much they loved you)," "No words, only love," and "I am here."

If you show your love through time, companionship may be a welcome gift for your friend. Do a puzzle together, go to a movie, or start a television series that you watch weekly. Find a regular day each week or month to gather for coffee, dinner, or a walk. Extend invitations so they feel included but give them the option to pass if they aren't feeling up for it. Keep showing up for them, week after week, month after month, year after year.

Refrain from offering advice or suggestions unless they ask. Avoid sentiments that aim to pull the person out of pain, such as, "You are strong," "God would never give you more than you can handle," "I know just how you feel," "Time heals all wounds," or "They're not suffering anymore." Don't begin any sentence with "At least . . ." like "At least you have other children," or "At least you're young and can find love again."

Instead of asking "How are you?" which can feel like a big question to answer, ask, "How has the morning been for you?" You might think to say, "I can't imagine how this feels for you." However, this phrase doesn't form a connection but rather puts distance between you and the person who is grieving. Help them feel supported with messages of connection and comfort like, "I'm here for you."

You don't need to fill the spaces with words. Your silent presence is often all they need. Hold space to hear whatever they want to say when they're ready. Acknowledge the enormity of their loss, now and always. It's natural to want to tell your own story or someone else's to make a connection, but this often burdens those who are grieving. Simply sit in their sorrow and validate their words.

Ask if they would like you to research available support in your area for them such as a grief support group, a yoga class or an art group specializing in loss, or a grief counselor. Present them with choices as they find their healing resources.

Don't stop asking questions about their loved one, and keep saying their name. Share your memories, even if you've shared them before, and ask to see photos. Bring their person into the present moment by asking, "What would _____ (their name) think of this?"

As your friend who is grieving faces holidays, birthdays, and death anniversaries, ask them how they want to spend the day and honor their wishes. Keep them in your thoughts and be especially attentive to their needs on both the day and the days leading up to it. A simple text like, "I'm thinking of you on _____ (their loved one's name) birthday today," communicates that you know this may be a tough day, and you are remembering their loved one with them.

If you wanted to help but now time has passed and you're unsure what to do, don't worry that you are reaching out too late. Kindness and empathy from various companions over time provide layers of comfort, offering grievers long-term support.

As you care for your friend or family member, continue to nurture yourself. To be with a griever and to hold their pain alongside them requires emotional energy. Eat well, rest, take breaks, hydrate, and move your body with walks outdoors. You will be a better companion when you tend to your own needs. Your full presence as you care for yourself offers the compassionate space they need as they heal.

THE FEELINGS WHEEL

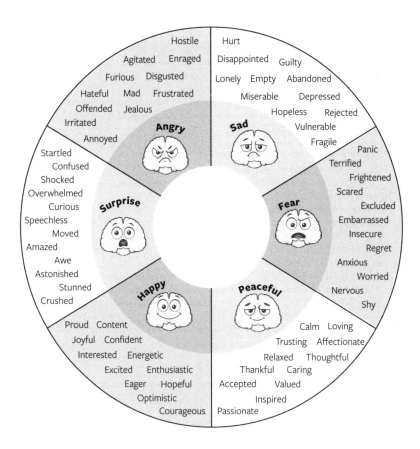

NOTES

Chapter 1 The Early Days

1. Kerry J. Ressler, "Amygdala Activity, Fear, and Anxiety: Modulation by Stress," *Biological Psychiatry* 67, no. 12 (2010): 1117–19.

2. Ian A. Clark and Clare E. Mackay, "Mental Imagery and Post-Traumatic Stress Disorder: A Neuroimaging and Experimental Psychopathology Approach to Intrusive Memories of Trauma," *Frontiers in Psychiatry* 6 (2015): 104.

3. Andy McNiel and Pamela Gabbay, *Understanding and Supporting Bereaved Children: A Practical Guide for Professionals* (New York: Springer, 2018), 16–17.

4. Jonathan M. Adler and Hal E. Hershfield, "Mixed Emotional Experience Is Associated with and Precedes Improvements in Psychological Well-Being," *PLoS ONE* 7, no. 4 (April 23, 2012): e35633.

Chapter 2 Opening to Your Sorrow

1. C. S. Lewis, *A Grief Observed* (New York: HarperCollins, 2001), 3.

2. Barbara Brown Taylor, *Learning to Walk in the Dark: Because God Often Shows Up at Night* (New York: HarperOne, 2014), 129.

3. Ann-Marie Widström et al., "Skin-to-Skin Contact the First Hour after Birth, Underlying Implications and Clinical Practice," *Acta Paediatrica* (Oslo, Norway: 1992) 108, no. 7 (July 2019): 1192–204.

4. Rachel Naomi Remen, *My Grandfather's Blessings: Stories of Strength, Refuge, and Belonging* (New York: Penguin, 2001), 38.

5. Amanda W. Baker et al., "The Role of Avoidance in Complicated Grief: A Detailed Examination of the Grief-Related Avoidance Questionnaire (GRAQ) in a Large Sample of Individuals with Complicated Grief," *Journal of Loss and Trauma* 21, no. 6 (February 2016): 533–47.

6. Alan Wolfelt, *A Child's View of Grief: A Guide for Parents, Teachers, and Counselors* (Fort Collins, CO: Companion Press, 2004), 12.

Chapter 3 When You're Grieving Your Partner

1. Alan Wolfelt, *Understanding Your Grief: Ten Essential Touchstones for Finding Hope and Healing Your Heart*, 2nd ed. (Fort Collins, CO: Companion Press, 2021), 32.

2. Margaret Stroebe et al., "Guilt in Bereavement: The Role of Self-Blame and Regret in Coping with Loss," *PLoS ONE* 9, no. 5 (May 12, 2014): e96606.

Chapter 4 When You're Grieving Your Child

1. Lori Cuthbert and Douglas Main, "Orca Mother Drops Calf, After Unprecedented 17 Days of Mourning," *National Geographic*, August 13, 2018, https://www.national geographic.com/animals/article/orca-mourning-calf-killer-whale-northwest-news.

2. Catherine H. Rogers et al., "Long-Term Effects of the Death of a Child on Parents' Adjustment in Midlife," *Journal of Family Psychology* 22, no. 2 (2008): 203–11.

3. Cambridge Dictionary, s.v. "Sehnsucht," accessed August 3, 2023, https://dictionary.cambridge.org/dictionary/german-english/sehnsucht.

4. Edward Hirsch, "Gabriel: A Poem," Edward Hirsch, accessed July 29, 2023, https://www.edwardhirsch.com/gabriel-a-poem-2/.

5. Rachel Ehmke, "Helping Children Deal with Grief," Child Mind Institute, February 20, 2023, https://childmind.org/article/helping-children-deal-grief/.

6. Ann Whiston-Donaldson, *Rare Bird: A Memoir of Loss and Love* (New York: Crown Publishing, 2015), 217.

7. Stephanie Frogge, "The Myth of Divorce Following the Death of a Child," Tragedy Assistance Program Survivors, March 1, 2015, https://www.taps.org/articles/21-1/divorce.

Chapter 5 Honoring Your Connection

1. Frederick Buechner, "Remember," Frederick Buechner, accessed August 20, 2023, https://www.frederickbuechner.com/quote-of-the-day/2021/1/16/remember.

2. Ted Rynearson, "Like an Amputation," Speaking Grief, accessed April 29, 2024, https://speakinggrief.org/experts/ted-rynearson.

3. Wolfelt, *Understanding Your Grief*, 31.

4. Dennis Klass, Phyllis R. Silverman, and Steven L. Nickman, eds., *Continuing Bonds: New Understandings of Grief* (New York: Routledge, 1996), 85.

5. Mitch Albom, *Tuesdays with Morrie: An Old Man, a Young Man, and Life's Greatest Lesson* (New York: Doubleday, 1997), 174.

6. Wolfelt, *Child's View of Grief*, 12.

7. Katherine C. Nordal, "Grief: Coping with the Loss of Your Loved One," American Psychological Association, January 1, 2020, https://www.apa.org/topics/families/grief.

Chapter 6 Finding Your Community

1. Donna Schuurman, *Never the Same: Coming to Terms with the Death of a Parent* (New York: St. Martin's, 2003), 40.

Chapter 7 Grief and Belief

1. C. Michael Hawn, "History of Hymns: 'It Is Well with My Soul,'" Discipleship Ministries, June 29, 2023, https://www.umcdiscipleship.org/resources/history-of-hymns-it-is-well-with-my-soul.

Chapter 8 The Weather of Your Grief

1. Daniel J. Siegel, *The Developing Mind: Toward a Neurobiology of Interpersonal Experience* (New York: Guilford Press, 1999), 253–54.

2. Siegel, *Developing Mind*, 254–55.

3. Siegel, *Developing Mind*, 256–58.

4. Siegel, *Developing Mind*, 253–55.

5. Gabor Maté, "Helper Syndrome, When Are We Enough?," *Psychotherapy Networker* (September/October 2021), 38–41, https://www.psychotherapynetworker.org/article/helper-syndrome.

6. "How to Do the 4-7-8 Breathing Exercise," Cleveland Clinic, September 25, 2022, https://health.clevelandclinic.org/4-7-8-breathing.

Chapter 9 Grief in Your Body

1. Bruce S. McEwen, "Allostasis, Allostatic Load, and the Aging Nervous System: Role of Excitatory Amino Acids and Excitotoxicity," *Neurochemical Research* 25, nos. 9/10 (October 2000): 1219–31.

2. Anna Braniecka, Ewa Trzebińska, Aneta Dowgiert, and Agata Wytykowska, "Mixed Emotions and Coping: The Benefits of Secondary Emotions," *PLoS ONE* 9, no. 8 (August 2014): e103940.

3. Shauna Niequist, *Bittersweet: Thoughts on Change, Grace, and Learning the Hard Way* (Grand Rapids: Zondervan, 2010), 232.

4. Leo Newhouse, "Is Crying Good for You?," *Harvard Health* (blog), March 1, 2021, https://www.health.harvard.edu/blog/is-crying-good-for-you-2021030122020.

5. Asmir Gračanin, Lauren M. Bylsma, and Ad J. J. M. Vingerhoets, "Is Crying a Self-Soothing Behavior?," *Frontiers in Psychology* 5, no. 502 (May 2014), https://doi.org/10.3389/fpsyg.2014.00502.

6. Jill Bolte Taylor, *My Stroke of Insight: A Brain Scientist's Personal Journey* (New York: Penguin, 2008), 128.

7. Peter A. Levine with Ann Frederick, *Waking the Tiger: Healing Trauma* (Berkeley, CA: North Atlantic Books, 1997), 97–98.

Chapter 10 Expressing Your Grief Through the Arts

1. Cathy A. Malchiodi, ed., *Creative Interventions with Traumatized Children* (New York: Guilford Press, 2008), 18–19.

2. Cathy Malchiodi, "With respect for my colleague Dan Siegel who coined 'name it to tame it,' expressive arts therapy and body-based interventions approach restorative communication differently," LinkedIn post, April 9, 2023, https://zw.linkedin.com/posts/cathymalchiodi_playmatters-expressyourself-expressiveartstherapy-activity-7050919584354222080-cgt5.

3. Malchiodi, *Creative Interventions*, 269.

4. American Music Therapy Association, "Music Therapy in Response to Crisis and Trauma," pdf, October 1, 2023, https://www.musictherapy.org/assets/1/7/MT_Crisis_2006.pdf.

5. Tamaki Amano and Motomi Toichi, "The Role of Alternating Bilateral Stimulation in Establishing Positive Cognition in EMDR Therapy: A Multi-Channel Near-Infrared Spectroscopy Study," *PloS ONE* 11, no. 10 (October 2016): e0162735.

6. Levine with Frederick, *Waking the Tiger*, 117–18.

Chapter 12 Returning to Work and School

1. Newhouse, "Is Crying Good for You?"

2. Steve Bender, "Short Naps at the Right Time of Day Can Have Myriad Benefits," Texas A&M Today, August 29, 2023, https://today.tamu.edu/2023/08/29/short-naps-at-the-right-time-of-day-can-have-myriad-benefits/.

3. Thomas Buckley et al., "Physiological Correlates of Bereavement and the Impact of Bereavement Interventions," *Dialogues in Clinical Neuroscience* 14, no. 2 (June 2012): 129–39.

4. Muriel A. Hagenaars, Emily A. Holmes, Fayette Klaassen, and Bernet Elzinga, "Tetris and Word Games Lead to Fewer Intrusive Memories When Applied Several Days after Analogue Trauma," *European Journal of Psychotraumatology* 8, suppl. 1 (October 2017): 1386959.

5. Dana R. Carney, Amy J. C. Cuddy, and Andy J. Yap, "Power Posing: Brief Nonverbal Displays Affect Neuroendocrine Levels and Risk Tolerance," *Psychological Science* 21, no. 10 (2010): 1363–68.

Chapter 14 Grieving Secondary Losses

1. Kelly Corrigan, *Glitter and Glue: A Memoir* (New York: Random House, 2014), 46.

Chapter 15 When Complexities Impact Grief

1. National Alliance for Children's Grief, "Supporting Children Grieving a Substance-Use Related Death," accessed May 1, 2024, https://indd.adobe.com/view/c2339eb6-de38-4478-ba76-1eb8b664db95.

2. Bessel A. van der Kolk, *The Body Keeps the Score: Brain, Mind, and Body in the Healing of Trauma* (New York: Penguin, 2015), 81.

3. Amano and Toichi, "Role of Alternating Bilateral Stimulation in Establishing Positive Cognition in EMDR Therapy."

Chapter 16 Enlarging Your Soul

1. Brené Brown, *Rising Strong: The Reckoning. The Rumble. The Revolution* (New York: Random House, 2015), 121.

2. Elisabeth Kübler-Ross, "Quotes," Elisabeth Kübler-Ross Foundation, accessed January 15, 2024, https://www.ekrfoundation.org/elisabeth-kubler-ross/quotes/.

3. Viktor E. Frankl, *Man's Search for Meaning* (Boston: Beacon Press, 2006), 54–55, 83–84, 115.

4. Albert Camus, "Return to Tipasa (1954)," accessed May 1, 2024, https://edder.org/literatura/tipasa3.pdf.

5. As quoted in Beth DeCarbo, "How Trauma Can Become a Catalyst for Personal Growth," *Wall Street Journal*, September 23, 2023, https://www.wsj.com/health/wellness/trauma-therapy-personal-growth-a120b276 (subscription required).

6. Charlyn Harper Browne, "The Strengthening Families Approach and Protective Factors Framework: A Pathway to Healthy Development and Well-Being," in *Innovative Approaches to Supporting Families of Young Children*, edited by Cheri J. Shapiro and Charlyn Harper Browne (New York: Springer, 2016), 1–24.

Supporting Your Child (Ages 0–12)

1. McNiel and Gabbay, *Understanding and Supporting Bereaved Children*, 16–17.

ERIN LEIGH NELSON

is the founder and executive director of Jessica's House, a grief support center for children and families. She first entered the grief world when her husband, Tyler, died in a midair collision in 1995 while on a fishing trip with his friends in Alaska. In the years after Tyler's death, Erin learned the importance of grief support for children and teens through two other tragic losses, including the suicide of her mom, which left her to support her fifteen-year-old sister alongside her own two young children. She began writing on child loss when she lost her son, Carter, in a car accident in 2019.

Erin is an advanced certified trauma practitioner through the National Institute for Trauma and Loss in Children and has been supporting families in grief for over twenty years. She is considered a valued resource in her community for those who have experienced the death of a spouse or child, but her favorite part of her job is serving in support groups with the littles at Jessica's House. She is a resource to the media and mental health professionals in assisting families after a tragedy. She often writes and speaks on best practices for supporting grieving children and families.

Erin lives in California's Central Valley with her husband, Bryan, and their children and grandchildren.

CONNECT WITH ERIN:

🌐 JessicasHouse.org
f Erin Leigh Nelson
⬡ @erinleighnelson
𝕏 @erinleigh47

COLLEEN E. MONTAGUE, LMFT,

is a licensed marriage and family therapist with over ten years of experience working with individuals and families. Her passion for grief support began early in her career.

Colleen is the program director for Jessica's House. Her role as a facilitator for parents who are grieving the death of their partner or child inspires her writing on grief support for families, as they teach her common themes and the unique ways they find healing. Colleen writes resources and speaks on best practices for grief support to educators, first responders, and mental health professionals.

Colleen lives in the Central Valley of California with her husband, Christian, and their children.

CONNECT WITH COLLEEN:

 JessicasHouse.org

JESSICA'S HOUSE

Jessica's House opened in April 2012 in the Central Valley of California and provides support in a safe place for children, teens, young adults, and their families who are grieving a death. Its inception was inspired by founder Erin Nelson, along with a group of community members who experienced untimely deaths in their families. Jessica's House is modeled after the Dougy Center, the first center in the United States to offer peer support for children grieving a loss.

Jessica's House extends the mission of EMC Health, Inc., and its parent organization, Covenant Ministries of Benevolence, offering support, resources, and comfort to those in need.

To learn more about Jessica's House, and for additional grief support resources, go to JessicasHouse.org.